Journey to God's House

An inside story of life at the World Headquarters

of Jehovah's Witnesses in the 1980s

A Memoir

By Brock Talon

Journey to God's House by Brock Talon

This book is a memoir. It contains the author's present recollections of his experiences since childhood that have been described to the best of his ability, without any purposeful intent of altering factual occurrences. Certain names and identifying characteristics of persons depicted may have been changed. Certain incidents may have been compressed or reordered. Certain conversations may have been paraphrased.

Brock Talon Enterprises

Copyright © 2013 Brock Talon

Revised January 1, 2018

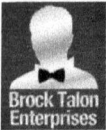

ISBN-13: 978-0615850528

ISBN-10: 0615850529

This book is dedicated to all Jehovah's Witnesses, past or present, who have borne experiences similar to mine. It is my hope that in reading the story of my journey, you will take solace in knowing that you are not alone in yours.

★

This book is also dedicated to my wife - my best friend and soul mate - who listened intently to all the original stories of my journey, gave me feedback on them, and encouraged me to complete this work. Like my life, this book is complete because of her.

TABLE OF CONTENTS:

Prologue

The stories you are about to read are true. The names have been changed to protect the innocent.

Well, sometimes the guilty too.

Brock Talon is not my real name. As an ex-Jehovah's Witness, I did not want to use my actual name because writing this memoir of my own journey could actually cause me trouble.

Yeah, it's like that.

You see, Jehovah's Witnesses do not appreciate people telling inside information to outsiders about what it is really like to be a many decades long member, and sometimes they can be quite vindictive about it. This is especially true if you have been a part of their elite class, and lived and worked at the center of their religious world in the Brooklyn, New York headquarters like I did. It is this headquarters that we called Bethel, meaning "House of God," that is also the center of my journey depicted in these writings.

By not using my real name I can also be frank about my own shortcomings and embarrassments. I can tell the tales that I would not have otherwise been brave enough to relate.

I do not bear animosity for the people depicted in these pages, but neither will I give them a pass on the distressing things I experienced at their hands. This is simply about me telling my own story as I remember it, unfiltered, pulling no punches. Still, these stories are not all negative accounts either. That is because I want to tell about the good and the bad I experienced living as a young person in that extraordinary place called Bethel.

Since this narrative is set in the early 1980s, it lends to a unique perspective on things, especially regarding how the culture of that day intertwined with and affected the life of the average young Jehovah's Witness. It also affords me the opportunity to look back many decades with 20/20 hindsight as to how well the moral values and prophetic utterances of the Jehovah's Witness faith fared over the years.

These eye-opening accounts are written for everyone. They will be entertaining and informative even if you have never been a Jehovah's Witness, or if you know very little about these unique people. So, if you are not all that well informed about Jehovah's Witnesses, then these chronicles will help give you insight on what makes them tick.

These stories are also for current Jehovah's Witnesses, and even ones who no longer practice the faith, as well as anyone who may think they know all there is to know about this religion. If this is you, trust me, you probably don't know everything. After all, how many of you actually lived in the headquarters at Bethel, or know someone who left that "Holy House of God" and is willing to tell you what it was really like to have lived there, without whitewashing it?

My guess, however, is that those souls who have lived at Bethel like me, are the ones who will appreciate these accounts the most. For those fellow soldiers, I think they will laugh and cry along with me as we all reminisce about our "journey to God's House."

Let's get this out of the way: you simply don't matter

I was a young man flying in a jet plane on my way to work and live at the World Headquarters of Jehovah's Witnesses in Brooklyn, New York, back in the early 1980s. I was thinking about *Dig Dug,* the newest video game that just came out. I had been trying to get a high score on it at the arcade near my home, but I never got the chance to play it very much. Little did I know, I would never play it again in that particular arcade because by the time I returned home, it would be closed, and *Dig Dug* wouldn't be the hot new game to play anymore. I'd be jobless and broke anyway, so it wouldn't matter much since I'd have no quarters to feed the machine. Such is the way many Jehovah's Witnesses return from Bethel: unemployed, penniless, alone, disoriented, and trying to figure out what to do next after their journey to God's House was apparently over.

Yes, I was a Jehovah's Witness. We were also known as "Witnesses" or "JWs." We Witnesses named our headquarters Bethel, which translates in Hebrew to "House of God." Being asked to work there was the ultimate privilege a young Witness could aspire to. There simply was no higher calling for anybody raised in the Jehovah's Witness faith. Every religion has a special holy place which is revered and where its believers plan to make the occasional pilgrimage: Islam has its Mecca, Judaism its Wailing Wall, Catholicism its Vatican, and hedonists the Playboy Mansion.

We Witnesses had Bethel.

Sure, we could be missionaries or we could work as special "servants" sent out to lead other JWs. However, Bethel service was the most prestigious "privilege" of them all. To work at Bethel was the Holy Grail of JW assignments, better than all those other things. There were various satellite Bethel locations in different countries, but the crown jewel location was in Brooklyn, New York, where the ultimate leaders of the Jehovah's Witness organization lived. We called our leaders "The Governing Body," or sometimes simply "GB." Those dozen or so older men ran the religion and every person in it from Bethel with an iron fist, as they claimed a direct authority from Jehovah God Himself. Millions of Jehovah's Witnesses followed every word written and spoken by those men. Bethel was the place where all of the literature was written and most of the literature was printed that supported the Jehovah's Witness faith. It's where all of the doctrine and dogma was enforced for the entire world. So here I was, headed to meet these giants... to get to know them personally and to work with them side by side! An awesome proposition! This would be like a young musician working with his childhood music idols but only better, because music idols don't get their mojo straight from God Himself. Being at Bethel made me a "Bethelite," the coolest thing you could be.

Growing up as a Jehovah's Witness, I was fairly ordinary by general Witness standards. My guess is that to those who are not JWs, all JWs are pretty ordinary to begin with. I mean, you very seldom hear about JWs who make much of themselves in the world. When they do, they are like Michael Jackson or Prince who make far too much of a spectacle of themselves. It seems to be either one extreme or another when it comes to JWs and how the rest of the world sees them.

Actually though, there are some famous Jehovah's Witnesses who many people do not realize were Witnesses at all. Take President Eisenhower for example. He was raised a JW, but later left the faith. This was the case with Geri Halliwell from the music group *Spice Girls* and the comedians the Wayans brothers as they too left the faith of their youth. However, among those who stayed true to their faith, at least as far as I know, are the Williams sisters of tennis fame, the musicians George Benson and Larry Graham, as well as the Latin singer Selena. So, you see, it is possible to be famous and to be a Jehovah's Witness (or ex-Witness) without having to necessarily be a strange bird.

As for me, I don't think I was particularly strange, nor was any member of my family. We were all pretty ordinary. My father was not an elder in our congregation, so this meant we had no real standing in our faith. An elder was someone who held a measure of power in the congregation as a leader of it, and power is something my family never saw. My mother never "pioneered" either, which is what a lot of the women did in the JW faith to give them standing. Pioneering was when a person dedicated a large amount of time to the door to door preaching work JWs are famous for. By and large, women did this more so than men. The name "pioneer" is meant to evoke the days when people opened up new territories in the early time of our country. This was done by the brave, rugged people of our nation's early history. Nowadays, the only new territory JW pioneers might open up is taking up a seat in the new coffee shop on the local street corner. Their pioneering would be accomplished by the many coffee breaks they would take while trying to artificially stretch out the time they were required to report to the elders, who in turn would report that time to Bethel.

I remember back when I pioneered, the lengths we would all go to bide our time while "out in field service" doing our preaching. It's comical to me now when I look back on it - we really just made up time to report, often doing nothing in particular but driving around. It's not that I could blame us for just passing the time, we were bored because the work was tedious. Most of the pioneers I knew didn't really seem to give a hoot about the people they were preaching to, although they tried hard to fake it. They really only looked to claim that preaching time on their timecard to keep their status as pioneers. Why do I say that? Well, I remember when the Jehovah's Witness leaders changed the rules saying you could count your time as "field service" time if you spent any time with a "weak" Jehovah's Witness who was inactive in the faith. So, counting this time was not just about trying to preach to strangers anymore because now you could count time talking to JWs who had stopped attending JW meetings. Suddenly, the number of visits to see these "weak and inactive" JWs by many of the "strong and active" JWs shot up all over the world. Before that, when it came to those losers who stopped attending JW meetings, it was pretty much "out of sight out of mind" as far as most JWs were concerned. However, once Witnesses could count that time on their timecards, well, suddenly the "love" kicked in and the visits to those lost souls started happening with earnest.

My family didn't have any other relatives in the JW faith, nor did we have a long history of being JWs with many generations passing on the baton to other generations. No, we didn't have any of those things. They were considered prestigious criteria by Jehovah's Witnesses, so my family basically had peon status. Non-JWs may not realize it, but there is a pecking order among JWs. My family unfortunately had a very small beak.

My own personal background was fairly nondescript as I was a JW who spent much of my time chasing girls and getting into trouble with them. (Yes. JWs get horny too. We just didn't do as much about it as everybody else.) Due to this, not many people in my Kingdom Hall thought I would amount to much in the Witness world. A Kingdom Hall (sometimes just called a "Hall") was what we called the building we worshipped in. We didn't call it a church because the Bible was clear that the word "church" referred to people, not a building. So, like everything else JWs did, we bucked tradition and called our building a Kingdom Hall since it was a meeting hall where people talked about the Kingdom of God.

(Interesting note: Even though JWs claimed that the Bible was clear that "church" meant people and not a building, we never used the word "church" in any way whatsoever. We didn't like that word because, well, everybody else used it, so we didn't. We Witnesses always had to be different.)

Things changed as I got older and I wanted to be a better Witness. I wanted to grow up and be serious about my faith. Mainly though, I simply didn't want to die at Armageddon in a hail of fire and brimstone which I was sure would be my fate if I felt up just one more "nice" Witness girl. So, I applied myself to following all the right Witness rules like keeping away from girls' bra straps. I kept my nose clean, did all the right Witness things, and soon I was accepted to go to Bethel. Wow! I had beaten the odds and triumphed over the naysayers who had doubted my spiritual conviction!

At this point, I was a very happy young man sitting in a coach class seat on my way to New York City. I was thinking about the wonderful hero's send-off I received from my home congregation where everyone was proud of me for getting accepted to work at God's House. They threw me a party, and baked cookies for me. They gave me presents, sage wisdom, and unasked for advice. The girls in the congregation said they would miss me and would write to me. My parents, however, showed mixed feelings, as they thought I was going through a "phase" and would soon come to my senses. They never were that "into" the JW religion to begin with, and quitting college to go to Bethel was ill-advised as far as they were concerned. Yet publically, they feigned pride in what I was doing, as that was the politically correct thing for them to do as Jehovah's Witnesses. As for me, I thought I was finally starting to make something of myself spiritually after years of struggle and screw-ups. I felt I was no longer a boy who never amounted to much as a Witness. It appeared that life was now going good for this Witness boy.

I had not traveled all that often back in those days, so the plane ride was a little uncomfortable. It was also strange to have packed away all my worldly belongings into four big bags. I remember asking myself, "Is that all I own?" I was thinking about my car that I sold because, after all, I couldn't afford to keep it and couldn't use it at Bethel. After praying, I got up, crammed myself into the little restroom on the airplane, and looked at myself in the bathroom mirror. There I saw this unfamiliar looking guy without a mustache staring back at me. The powers that be at Bethel told me to shave my mustache because, well, that's what you did there to be "extra" clean cut. JWs are clean cut to begin with, but we Bethelites evidently had to be even more so. So, I shaved my mustache, one that I had grown since I could grow one, feeling a bit like a naked sheep must feel after being freshly shorn. I thought back on how I also got rid of a lot of my stuff before I left home, giving my sibling some of it, and selling or giving away other stuff.

I also thought about the girls I liked back home who I probably would not be able to pursue any longer. "Well, maybe that is a good thing," I thought, trying to convince myself that totally keeping away from females would be the right thing to do. Little did I know that Bethel was not a good place for this kind of thinking, since it was visited every week by hoards of females looking for eligible males. As you will soon see, this proved to be a special burden on a guy like me who was trying to be good.

For my stay at Bethel I had some money saved, mostly from selling my car. I knew I had to make my money stretch for who knew how long due to the fact that Bethelites were paid very little. Bethelites basically worked for free at God's House. Heck, I even quit college to go there, which might have hurt me most of all. You see, Witnesses actually look down on other Witnesses who go to college. If I was going to be asked to go to Bethel, I needed to show "them" that I was a serious JW by avoiding worldly and selfish pursuits like college.

I told myself that all of this was the right thing to do because if I didn't go to Bethel now, I would never go, and I would regret it. If I didn't go now, I would just screw up and be lost. I wanted to be a better person and I wanted to help others in an unselfish way, which was new for me. Up until then, my life had been pretty much about me. I believed that the people at the World Headquarters were going to see after me, love me, nurture my spirituality, and make me a better person. Besides, they would also save me from myself so that I wouldn't die an unrepentant sinner. All Witnesses seem to live in constant guilt and worry about their future; I was no different. I thought Bethel would fix all that because, after all, it was God's House.

So, it was done. I was going. No looking back.

Someone from Bethel mailed me a welcome letter and asked if I needed to be picked up at the airport. I thought this was a good idea, so I called the main office and made arrangements for the pickup. I gave a description of myself and was told someone would be able to easily find me at the airport if I held up a *Watchtower* magazine and stood in a particular spot. My plane finally landed in New York. I got all my bags together and trudged over to the designated spot. Sheepishly, I held up a copy of the world famous Jehovah's Witness *Watchtower* magazine with a feeble smile. I waited and waited. My smile started to fade as my arm got tired. The *Watchtower* began drooping. One hour passed... then two.

After a number of hours, I had to drag my big bags around to find a cart. I couldn't find one. Dismayed, I dragged my bags to a pay phone. (We didn't have cell phones in those days.) I called the Bethel offices but couldn't get anybody on the phone who I had spoken to before as they were all out or busy. I told whoever was on the other end of the line that I was waiting at the airport. They responded to me that they knew that, and that I should just hold on and somebody would be there to get me.

So, I schlepped back to that spot and waited another hour or so.

Nobody came.

I was starting to really get upset by then and it was getting late in the day. So, I decided to take matters into my own hands. I dragged all my bags to a taxi. I didn't have much cash on me, but now I was forced to pay for a taxi to Brooklyn from LaGuardia Airport. I finally arrived at Bethel. I paid the driver most of my cash and dragged my bags into the main building of the headquarters of Jehovah's Witnesses, also known as 124 Columbia Heights.

When I finally got to the front desk, I was exhausted. Still, managing to summon up a smile, I spoke to the lady before me, "Hi. I'm Brock. I'm here!" ("Ta-da!" I said in my mind.) The lady there just kind of looked at me over her half-glasses like an irritated schoolmarm and asked, "What was your name again?" I told her yet another time, "I'm Brock... Brock Talon, the new Bethelite." Ta-da! I thought that surely they were eagerly anticipating the arrival of the famous Brock Talon, right? Everybody back at home knew me, so why didn't these people? After all, Bethel invited <u>me</u> to come, so how could they not know me and not be expecting me when I arrived?

The lady looked through some papers for a bit and shook her head. I was starting to feel anger now. What the heck? Didn't they have <u>any</u> record of me? The lady could see I was getting upset and then told me to hold on. She shuffled some more papers and then went and spoke with someone in another room. When she returned, she finally said something like, "Oh, yes, hmmm," and then called another person. She smiled for the first time, uttered a bland, "Welcome brother," and then gave me a key and some papers. She told me to follow the "brother" who appeared out of nowhere. JWs call each other "brother" and "sister" by the way, but I sure didn't feel like anybody's brother at that time. I felt more like an uninvited guest telling a surprised friend at his doorstep that I was moving into his house.

This "brother" put my stuff on a cart and led me through some tunnels, the walk felt like it went on for miles. There were people scurrying all about, nobody really smiling or noticing me at all. I realized then that Bethel was a maze of buildings, all owned by the Watch Tower Bible and Tract Society of New York. This was the legal entity that controlled all the property and belongings of the Jehovah's Witness religion and was often nicknamed "The Society" or sometimes called "The Organization." The maze of buildings we called Bethel that this legal entity owned was connected by tunnels beneath the streets of Brooklyn.

The tunnels made getting around Bethel easier, especially in inclement weather conditions. However, the tunnels had a bit of a dungeon like feel. Since everybody in the tunnels were all Jehovah's Witnesses, most of them Bethelites, there was no need to smile or pretend to care about anybody they saw there. They all just scurried about like ants doing what ants do. You wouldn't see ants stopping to tell each other, "Hey Mac. How's it going at the hill?" "Oh, very nice thank you. I'm on my way there with this beetle leg. How are you handling that dead cricket?" No, ants didn't bother with that chit chat, and neither did Bethelites.

So, here was my very first impression of Bethel, and it was kind of weird... kind of cold. To add to this oddness, the guy escorting me didn't talk much. He was robotic, and I remember wondering if everybody at Bethel was like this guy. After observing the clinical activity in the tunnels, I was beginning to think they were. We finally got to the building where I would live, which would have been many blocks away from where we started had we walked through the streets of Brooklyn rather than navigating the tunnels. We then had to take a long elevator ride to an upper floor of that JW owned residence building aptly nicknamed "The Towers." We finally got to my room. Brother Robot now said simply, "Here's your room." Looking back on this scene, it sort of reminds me of the line from the song *Hotel California*: "We are programmed to receive. You can check out any time you like, but you can never leave..."

Well, we got my bags into the room and he left with no real words spoken between us. The door closed behind him with a thud.

I was alone.

Now, I was young and not all that experienced in life, but I did know this: I had felt more welcomed simply checking into a hotel on a vacation. It was a shock that Bethel basically processed me like I was nobody. They didn't even pick me up at the airport when they promised to and didn't greet me when I arrived. Up until that moment, I thought I was somebody. My feelings were quite hurt by all this, as I guess I expected much more fan fare at my arrival, similar to the attention I got when I left home. It would only dawn on me later that I was only one of many thousands of young men working at Bethel at any given time, with dozens arriving each week replacing the dozens who leave each week. So, from their perspective, I actually was not that special at all. I would come to find out that I would just be another worker drone to them.

I looked at my bags and all my remaining material possessions lying there in a heap. I glanced out the window at an alien cityscape and heard the strange cacophony coming from the street. I finally realized that I was in a place where I didn't know anybody. It struck me too that I would be away from all my family, friends, pets, and familiar places for good. I had given up everything to be here and I suddenly missed everything that I left behind.

The enthusiasm I had felt for Bethel when I left home was suddenly replaced by trepidation. Given all I had sacrificed up to this point to get here and the pitiful reception I was just shown upon my arrival, I wondered, "Was this how I would be welcomed by everyone? Was <u>this</u> how I could expect to be treated from now on?"

As all of these emotions swept over me, I just sat on the bed and began to cry.

Enjoy your birthday cake son; it's going to be your last

Let me back up for a bit so I can tell you how I got to be a Jehovah's Witness in the first place, how I began my journey to find where God lives, and why I eventually made my way to the place called "The House of God."

When I was just a little guy back in the 1960s, I used to ask my mother all kinds of questions about many things. When I asked her how God could walk on the clouds and why He doesn't fall through them, she didn't know. Her church did little to teach her about the Bible, so she bought me some of those Seventh-day Adventist Bible story books you can find at some dentist's offices, and she read them to me. Those books would tide me over for a time and I loved them. Still, often times the more you learn about things, the more you realize how much you don't know. Some answers just lead to more questions. One day, I asked my mother another particularly puzzling question, probably something like how old God was, and she wasn't sure how to answer it. The answer wasn't in those books either.

On that fateful day there came a knock at the door, and lo and behold, it was a kindly older Jehovah's Witness woman who was offering a "free home Bible study." My mom jumped at this opportunity. Soon, the entire family was studying with Jehovah's Witnesses, which at first seemed safe and was pleasant enough. Jehovah's Witnesses are very nice to the people they are "studying" with. It isn't until later, once you learn and accept "The Truth," that things start to get intense and a bit unpleasant. JWs nickname their religion "The Truth" because of a little blue book they used to give out and study many years ago. This book was entitled *The Truth that Leads to Eternal Life*. After a while, JWs just called what they believed "The Truth," implying of course that everything else was not.

Well, about the time my parents became more serious about The Truth, I was coming up on my 6th birthday. At about the same time they planned my birthday party, they learned from their studies with that kindly older JW lady that celebrating birthdays was wrong. They learned from her that only wicked, self-centered, worldly, and pagan people celebrated them, certainly not "true Christians." You see, JWs call anyone who is not a JW worldly, because they are of the "world of Satan," while JWs are not. JWs also call anyone who is not a JW who claims to be a Christian a liar, as they are really part of "Babylon the Great" the "World Empire of False Religion" and are in fact a dupe of Satan. The only "true Christians" are JWs.

My parents were just learning all the new JW rules about sinful things like birthdays, and were in a quandary because they had already promised me a birthday party. So, they kept their promise and invited my friends over. They gave me a hat and balloons and a cake with candles. But, as I was having my party, my parents told me that I should enjoy it, because it was the last birthday party I would ever have.

It turned out that my parents becoming Jehovah's Witnesses would be a last for me in many things. It would be the last time I would celebrate Christmas, Easter, Halloween, The Fourth of July, and pretty much any holiday after that. It would be the last time I would salute the flag, watch a movie with a ghost in it, or use the word "luck." The number of restrictions that Jehovah's Witnesses put on their children, and on each other for that matter, is simply mind boggling. I cannot possibly tell you all of them here, but needless to say, life drastically changed for me as my 6th birthday party came to a close. I just didn't realize that fact yet, because at that moment I was just a clueless kid in a pointy hat with a kazoo happily eating birthday cake.

Looking back on it now, I realize that I had a hand in my parents becoming Jehovah's Witnesses. Had I not been so darn inquisitive about things like how many animals were actually on the ark, and why God didn't make room for the dinosaurs on it, well, I might have not ever seen the inside of a Kingdom Hall.

☆

Jehovah's Witnesses work very hard to make you a regular at the Kingdom Hall. They want you to become one of them, and will study the Bible with you using their special Bible literature for as long as it takes for you to get baptized in The Truth. Ironically, once you are baptized as a bona fide Jehovah's Witness, it actually becomes quite easy at that point to get booted out of the religion altogether!

One of the things Jehovah's Witnesses are infamous for is "disfellowshipping." This is done when you have sinned in such a way as to require punishment from the congregation. Then, the JWs all band together to kick you out of the congregation and refuse to speak to you, even if they were to happen to meet you on the street by chance. This is done out of love for you in order to save your miserable hide in the long run by shaming you into repentance, as well as to protect the rest of the congregation from your sorry example. It is the worst possible fate for a Witness because you are cut off from all of your JW friends, and also from your JW family as well. You see, if you are disfellowshipped (nicknamed "DF'd") then even your own Witness mother will not talk to you!

Now, as you might expect, JWs are pretty much sequestered from everyone in the world to begin with, because they are told everybody else is worldly and wicked and will die at Armageddon. So, they are instructed to keep their distance from everyone else, and have no real ties to anybody because of this, even other family members who are not JWs. But that also means that if a JW is DF'd, then they are one hundred percent completely alone in the world because they had previously cut all non-JWs from their lives. Also, as a JW, you don't even know how to act around people who are not JWs. You are handicapped in pretty much every imaginable way; so once DF'd, you find yourself a stranger in a strange non-JW land. This is a terrifying proposition to the average Jehovah's Witness.

I bring this up because one of the surest ways to get DF'd is to commit a sexual sin. Natural heterosexual encounters, a young unmarried man with a young unmarried woman for example, is called fornication, and if you did it more than once as a JW you most likely would be DF'd for it. The Bible strictly forbids fornication, along with adultery, greediness, drunkenness, reviling, extortion, lying, thievery, cowardice, faithlessness, and more. But for some reason, Jehovah's Witnesses have a special aversion to sexual sin. I could never figure out why sex was a worse sin compared to the others.

I can give you a number of examples of why I say this by simply contemplating the sins listed in the Bible that Jehovah's Witnesses use to disfellowship their own. For example, 1 Corinthians 6: 9,10, says: "Do not be deceived; neither fornicators, nor idolaters, nor adulterers, nor effeminate, nor homosexuals, nor thieves, nor the greedy, nor drunkards, nor revilers, nor swindlers, will inherit the kingdom of God."

Also, consider Revelation 21:8, which reads: "But as for the cowardly, the faithless, the detestable, as for murderers, the sexually immoral, sorcerers, idolaters, and all liars, their portion will be in the lake that burns with fire and sulfur, which is the second death."

Jehovah's Witnesses point to these scriptures to show that fornicators, or those involved in a variety of sexual sin, deserve this disfellowshipping punishment. OK, fine. But what about the other sins listed in these same scriptures? Do Jehovah's Witnesses take these sins as seriously? Let's consider:

Revilers: *Persons who use abusive speech, who scorn or use profanity against another*

I grew up seeing brothers in the JW congregation revile people all the time. I've even seen some elders act in this manner. It was well known, for example, that even a few of the presidents of the Watch Tower Bible and Tract Society itself were given to bursts of anger and to reviling. They often treated the Bethelites like cattle by yelling, cursing, and name calling. Still, this kind of behavior was ignored because, well, that's just the way these people were. If they had bad tempers, we were expected to be forgiving of our brothers who took the lead but had that kind of abusive speech. They were only human after all. They didn't mean to do it and really had good hearts, right?

For the record, <u>I've never once heard of a single JW being DF'd for being a reviler.</u> Not once. But I've seen over the years many who practiced it, including elders and Ministerial Servants, that is, the people who lead the individual Jehovah's Witness congregations.

Greedy people: *Persons showing intense selfish desire for things, especially related to food*

I've seen elder's wives who were huge 400 pound monsters and who gobbled up everything in sight like Jabba the Hutt on a binge. Yet these ladies were never deemed by other JWs as "greedy" at all. No sir. You see, it would be explained that they had a "glandular" problem, so it was overlooked.

For the record, I've never heard of a single JW being DF'd for being greedy. I have, however, known far too many who were not just greedy regarding food, but in other ways too, like with money. Still, this was simply never enforced in a JW congregation. I defy anyone to show me an example of some JW being DF'd for this particular sin.

Drunkards: *Persons frequently or habitually drunk*

I've seen many a JW couple who loved to have that wine every day, often times glass after glass until they were all giggly and silly. Were they punished as drunkards? No. You see, it was deemed that this was not drunkenness, it was just being "happy." No punishment was given to them for this either. It didn't matter that they might have received a DUI conviction on their records; it was to be overlooked as long as nobody complained about it in the congregation. As a matter of fact, most young Bethelites themselves drank far too much, which I will tell more about later.

Now, I admit that I have seen a <u>few</u> JWs DF'd for drunkenness. However, this was rare and only in the most extreme of cases, and it certainly was not just because somebody got drunk once or twice. I always thought this issue was particularly odd because to a Jehovah's Witness, should a person get drunk once or twice, on occasion that is, they would never think to label this person a "drunkard" and punish them for it. But should a person have sex outside marriage once or twice, they would immediately be labeled a "fornicator," punished, and then whispered about for years.

Thieves (swindlers): *Persons who take what is not theirs or cheat others out of what is theirs*

I've seen elders and their wives (or others in a congregation) "borrow" money and not pay it back. This wasn't usually deemed "stealing" if those people happened to be "in need" and had a hard time paying it back. The other JW was expected to just accept losing that money out of "love for their brother." Also, it was almost always forbidden to ever take another JW to court and sue them. Even if you were the injured party in such a situation, you could get into trouble yourself with the congregation elders for suing another brother. It was thought to be disgraceful to the JW faith to have one Witness sue another Witness. So, you were expected to "work it out" with that brother or sister who borrowed money from you. In the end, if they didn't pay, well, too bad. You usually were expected to eat the loss and live and learn.

It was very rare that a brother was DF'd for cheating another or for stealing outright for that matter. It might happen from time to time, but I never saw it much, except, ironically at Bethel. You see, if a person in a regular congregation got cheated or stolen from, the general attitude was that the injured party should forgive that person and "work it out" with them. But should somebody cheat or steal from Bethel, well, they were immediately ejected from Bethel. Also, pressure would be put on the person's home congregation elders to do some sort of congregational judiciary action against them once they got home.

Liars: Persons who do not tell the truth or who bend or twist the truth

I've seen JWs who were compulsive liars as well, yet nothing was done about that at all. Often times this habit was just laughed at as they were deemed "colorful people." Those forgiving Jehovah's Witness leaders in the congregation would say things like, "Oh, you know how so and so is. Don't take him so seriously... ha ha." So, again for the record, I've never heard of a single JW being DF'd for being a liar, although I've known many who practiced it compulsively.

I could go on with the other "deadly" sins too, like the cowardly, the faithless, and so on. For the sake of time I'll just move on.

In conclusion, JWs don't enforce any real punishment for many of these sins that I just mentioned. I saw all kinds of these particular sins practiced by JWs I knew in many of the congregations I attended over the years. I saw these sins practiced <u>all the time</u> without any real repercussions for them. It was evident that many JWs did things that the Bible clearly said we should not do, things which were listed in scriptures *right next to the words "fornicators" (or "the sexually immoral")* but these non sex related sins were most often times just ignored, brushed aside, or at most, addressed in a milquetoast way.

☆

Now, this "ignoring of sin" was especially true if a person had power or standing in the congregation. Even sex sins could be forgiven if you were the son or daughter of an elder. These privileged people always got more chances than the nobodies like me.

I once knew an elder's son who was my age who was a ministerial servant in our congregation. This meant he had some status and privilege (think deacon in a church). Eventually he married. A few years after he was married, it came out that he had slept with his wife's mother before his wedding day. Not only that, he also kept this going for a short time afterwards, so he kept on having sex with his mother-in-law who was a pioneer in the congregation. Finally, after some time, he broke off the adultery, but these two prominent JWs did "practice" this sin for quite a while.

Still, the elders in his congregation didn't DF him. In fact, they didn't even take away his congregational privileges. This was unheard of in JW circles as usually you would get some sort of punishment for that kind of serious sin. These elders figured that he felt bad about what he did since he did stop doing it. Also, they reasoned, he had worked hard in the congregation since stopping his ongoing adultery with his mother-in-law. Well, this thinking by the elders broke all the JW rules I knew of. In most Kingdom Halls the offender would have at least been "privately reproved" (which was a sort of probationary period put on someone) and he would also have lost all of his congregational privileges, at a minimum. The fact that he slept with his own mother-in-law didn't even faze these elders. Neither did the fact that he did it many more times than once. It turned out, however, that his father was the highest ranking elder in his congregation and he ran it with an iron fist. The other elders just went along with this weak decision. You see, I often found that nepotism runs deep in the typical Jehovah's Witness Kingdom Hall. This last story is a perfect example of that.

Now, compare that to what would happen to somebody like me. Should you find yourself a teenage boy or girl and not be the child of an elder, and then have the gall to have sex, well, that wouldn't be tolerated. You would be warned once, and if you did the sin again, DF'd. If it came to the elders attention you had done this sex thing over a period of time, then you would be labeled a person who "practiced sin" and DF'd on the spot without any hesitation.

So, the DF'ing equation in the Witness world is simple: "Sex sin" + "Being a nobody" = "Your disfellowshipped butt"

Well, that was my fear - being disfellowshipped. I didn't smoke dope or cigarettes. I didn't gamble. I didn't fight with other kids or revile them. I never lied to anyone or cheated in school. I neither drank alcohol, nor cursed. I got straight A's in school and never caused my parents one bit of trouble in any way. I made my own bed, made my own lunches, had a part-time job, and made my own money to buy myself clothes and other things I needed. I was moderate in all my habits and exercised regularly. I helped out other brothers and sisters in the congregation when they needed me to, and was nice to everyone who came across my path, JW or otherwise. I worked in the congregation running microphones during the meetings, and helped clean the Kingdom Hall on a regular basis after the meetings and on weekends. My teachers liked me, my neighbors thought I was a nice kid, and I was kind to all my pets.

However, I had one very fatal flaw: I loved women and I loved sex. I liked everything about women and they liked me back. I was "cursed" as a JW because I had a naturally good physique. Also, I was considered to be of above average in looks by most, even handsome by many, and not just by JW girls, but by worldly girls too. It was easy to get attention from Witness girls because the Witness world was relatively small. In that world, I could be the proverbial big fish in the small pond. But I could also get attention from non-Witness girls as well, and this is where the danger was for me. I always craved attention from the opposite sex, and I always seemed to find it. That meant as a JW I was always finding trouble.

Well, this wouldn't do. As a JW, this surely was a straight ticket to destruction. I was always terrified that I would be DF'd. Heck, even if I wasn't caught and punished by the elders, then Armageddon would come and God would bring the end of me. I would be thrown into the Lake of Fire, penis first.

That little boy with his last birthday cake at six years old would grow up into a guilt-ridden Jehovah's Witness teen, worried of being labeled a sexual deviant just because he liked girls.

As a result, he tried his best to be what he thought was the JW equivalent of monkhood, that is, to volunteer to go to Bethel to get his spiritual act together and avoid women in order not to suffer the terrible fate of damnation by sex.

As you will soon see, this became an eye-opening and life changing event for that little boy, now grown into a young man physically, but still young at heart and emotionally naive. That little boy was about to grow up in ways he never dreamt of. This would happen by completely changing his life, leaving everything behind, and working and living at God's House.

In turn however, this life changing journey would take a terrible toll on his psyche.

A snowflake's chance in Hades

The day I found out I was accepted to go to God's House was a very strange day in many ways. It happened on the weekend of what Jehovah's Witnesses call a Circuit Assembly.

Witnesses get together for five meetings a week to study the Bible, besides gathering together to go out in field service to do the preaching work once a week. However, these were simply not enough meetings for us. No sir. We <u>also</u> met once a year in a larger assembly of a couple of dozen congregations in other nearby Kingdom Halls put together into what we called a Circuit, which was run by a special kind of elder called a Circuit Overseer. So, once a year this Circuit Overseer gathered us all together into an all-day-Saturday and all-day-Sunday Bible study fest called a Circuit Assembly.

(Side note: We also had an even <u>larger</u> annual assembly we called a District Convention, which was a group of Circuits, and was presided over by a District Overseer. The District Convention was an even longer Bible Study fest, which was more days than a Circuit Assembly. Nobody could say us JWs were lightweights when it came to getting together to study the Bible because we did it like nobody's business.)

While going to those assemblies might sound very boring to the non-Jehovah's Witness, it wasn't to us. It was exciting, especially for us younger folks, because there we could do what was most important in our lives: meet other young people to flirt with! You see, JWs have a fairly limited world in which to find other potential love interests, and these assemblies were key opportunities for this. Hence, we anxiously awaited them, often getting fresh haircuts or even buying new clothes and jewelry for these meetings on the chance we could find the love of our lives.

This particular Circuit Assembly was a few weeks after I handed in my Bethel application to the elders in my congregation. I made the mistake of telling one of my friends I had applied to Bethel, and soon this information got out to everybody else. Again, you have to understand that JWs live in a pretty small world; this means they often know a lot about each other, even if one didn't necessarily want those things known. It was sort of like living in a small town, but even worse than that because everybody in that town was also extremely nosy and judgmental.

At the time, I believed that many JWs who knew me thought I had a snowflake's chance in Hades at getting accepted to Bethel, but they were mostly too nice to say that to my face. So, they just said that to each other instead. This was made very clear to me by a guy I had never even met before. I was talking to some of my friends before the start of the assembly session that day, and this stranger walked up to me. The ensuing oddly disconcerting conversation went something like this:

Stranger: You're Brock, right?

Me: Uh, yes.

Stranger: One in ten.

Me: How's that?

Stranger: One in ten. That's your chances.

Me: My chances of what?

Stranger: Of being accepted to Bethel. It's a fact that only one out of every ten Bethel applicants is accepted. But of course, the ones usually accepted are long time full-time pioneers and are usually ministerial servants at least, if not elders.

Now, this stranger didn't even bother to introduce himself to me before he started in with his blather. What he did do was unload a whole boatload of JW nuance that was filled with the typical judgmental claptrap that Witnesses are so good at. He was staring at me with a stupid grin on his face, daring me to reply to what he just said. He said this to me in front of all of my friends by the way, which made it all the more awkward.

You non-Witnesses reading this probably won't get it. For those of you that don't understand the JW language, let me translate what he said. For starters, though, I should say up front that there is no "fact" about how many people are accepted to Bethel versus how many apply. When I lived there later on I asked about this issue to people at Bethel, that is, those who could really know how many are accepted versus how many are rejected. It turns out this kind of information is never published. Only the most important people in Bethel know the answer to this, and they certainly would not tell those figures to the likes of this stranger standing in front of me now. In fact, nobody I knew had this kind of information at all, so people just guessed.

But I digress. So now, let me explain the nuance of his words. What this guy was saying was that in order to get accepted to Bethel, you probably had to full-time pioneer, which meant in those days you spent ninety to one hundred hours per month in preaching work. Also, according to him, you should have been doing this for many years (a "long time pioneer"). He somehow knew that I only part-time pioneered, and had only been doing it for less than a year. Undoubtedly, he was making a dig at my short and spotty record of what JW's called "full-time service."

He also was making a dig at the fact I was not an elder in the congregation, and I was not an elder's helper, also known as a ministerial servant. I had never been given either of those JW honors, which he also evidently knew.

In conclusion, what he was saying to me was this: "It is very difficult to get into Bethel <u>even</u> if you were a long time pioneer, who you are not, and <u>even</u> if you were honored in other ways like being an elder, who we all know you are not either. So, you should forget about ever being accepted into Bethel, Brock, you presumptuous twit!"

Well, I just looked at this guy who was smirking at me, caught off guard at his attack for no apparent reason. I just gave a tepid response, saying something like, "Oh, OK. Well, thanks for letting me know." I walked away puzzled by this, with my friends in tow, as they tried to comfort me by saying things like, "Don't listen to him," and, "Who was that guy?" All I could think of was that I sure wish I hadn't told anybody I had applied to Bethel, because now I would be a laughing stock when I was rejected. I was also thinking I might see many jerks like the one who just confronted me come out of the woodwork this weekend to make fun of me. Even though my friends supported me, I knew they too secretly doubted that I would be accepted to Bethel.

This issue became more apparent to me because unfortunately for me, right after this I ran into Patty Pesty. Now, Patty was a girl I had a long history with. We never actually dated from my point of view. I thought we were just friends. But in her mind, we were meant to be together. An example of how she could be a pest was that she would go to my house and visit my family when I wasn't there. Then, when she was left alone, she would sneak into my bedroom and steal my underwear! She would subsequently tell all the other girls I might be interested in that we were secretly dating, also implying that we were fooling around. She would lend credibility to this assertion by showing them my underwear (the ones she stole) which she would be wearing!

Well, we were not dating and we were not fooling around either. I really wasn't interested in her at all because I thought she was a pest at best... crazy at worst. Besides, I liked a girl who had more curves than she had; I was not all that physically attracted to her. Patty was attractive to others, in that 1980s big-haired, skinny with small features and wearing oversized shoulder-padded clothes way. Many guys wanted to date her, but to my dismay, she only seemed to want me. Patty was causing me trouble, and she was getting on my last nerve.

Well, Patty Pesty came up to me at the assembly that weekend and said something like, "Hi Brock. How's that Bethel thing going for you? Ha Ha." She then walked off, looking at me over her bony shoulders, with what she thought were flirty eyes, thinking she was being clever and seductive, when in fact she was just being annoying. On this particular day, Patty was deciding to bust my hump about the very same issue Brother Stranger just confronted me with. I didn't realize it then, but there was a connection to both of these events. "Great," I thought. "Now this whole assembly weekend will be about people laughing at my stupidity for thinking I could be accepted to Bethel."

Well, it turned out that the day ended without any more drama, so I was relieved about that. When we got home I checked the mail, and would you believe it? There was a big fat envelope from the Watch Tower Bible and Tract Society addressed to me! I opened it excitedly and, yes, you guessed it, I was accepted to Bethel! The letter told me the date I should report to Bethel and gave other details about my upcoming stay there. Holy cow! My life had just changed! I couldn't wait to tell everyone. I knelt and prayed to Jehovah God, thanking Him for this opportunity.

The next day at the assembly I told the very first person I knew that I had been accepted to Bethel, and then another and then another. The news spread through the Circuit like wildfire. You see, we had very few people accepted to Bethel in this particular Circuit. Somehow, I had managed to do what few others had done in my local area. It was weird how I could tell that starting that day many JWs looked at me completely different. I was now given respect and treated better by some of the more aloof, pious and snooty JWs. Here the JW nobody, Brock Talon, was accepted to Bethel, a feat none of them ever achieved and none of their children achieved either. Most JWs never would. Out of millions of JWs, Brock Talon would hobnob with the Governing Body. Take that Brother Stranger, wherever you were, with that "one in ten" nonsense!

Well, I didn't have to wait long to run into Brother Stranger again. You see, I soon found out that Brother Stranger had a thing for Patty Pesty, and he was determined to "steal" her away from me. Patty had told him we were an item, but he was going to show her that he was the right man for her and not me. Unfortunately for me, I didn't have a clue I was in the middle of this bizarre infatuation triangle. Anyway, Brother Stranger boldly walked up to me and started yet another surreal conversation:

Stranger: Hey Brock. Why didn't you tell Patty you had been accepted to Bethel?

Me: Huh? What?

Stranger: She told me that you two are close, and yet you told a bunch of other people about it and never even told her. She had to find out about it second hand. That's pretty lousy.

Me: Well, I...

Stranger: She's in the bathroom right now crying. You need to go to her and comfort her.

With about a dozen people watching, I just stared at the guy, wondering what I would do. I still had no clue at that time who this guy was. It dawned on me that soon I would be at Bethel and all these people would be far away, including Brother Stranger and Patty Pesty. I had everybody's attention, and I figured for the time being I could do no wrong. After all, I was a Bethelite now! So, I said:

Me: [annoyed and a bit angry] Excuse me, but just who the heck <u>are</u> you?

Stranger: [stammering] Er... uh... I'm Joe. Joe Schmo. I'm Patty's friend.

Me: Well Joe, you're not <u>my</u> friend. Actually, I've never met you before in my life until yesterday when you told me my chances of going to Bethel were nil. Now that you find out I'm going to Bethel after all, you want to give me grief about how I choose to announce it.

Stranger: Uh... well, I'm trying...

Me: Look, if you are in fact Patty's friend, then I suggest you go find her and comfort her yourself and get out of my face. OK?

Stranger: [quietly] Um, OK. Sorry.

We all laughed and walked away from Brother Stranger, now known as Joe Schmo. At that moment, given everything, I felt like I had won the lottery. Not only was I going to Bethel and had quieted the naysayers about me, I had a new found power to shut jerks up like Joe Schmo because I was now higher up on the JW food chain.

Better yet, there was a snowflake's chance in Hades that I would ever have to deal with Patty Pesty or Joe Schmo again.

Those were odds I could get behind.

Big Tex

Let's get back to my Bethel story now. The day after my humiliating experience of being left at the airport and then unceremoniously dumped into my room, my journey continued as I found myself going to my first Bethel Class. I was joined by other new guys who would be part of what we called our "Bethel Group."

I remember sitting in the Bethel class with my Bethel group, eager to get started on my new Bethel life. This group was the source of some of my first friends at Bethel whose friendships would last long after the class ended. If one were lucky, you would have many cool guys in your Bethel group to get to know and hang out with, which I had. Every once in a while, you could even have (gasp!) a single girl in your Bethel group. Which, I also had. These were a rarity, since "single sisters" in Bethel lasted about as long as a giant cookie would near the Cookie Monster. They almost never lasted as single for very long, often getting engaged very quickly because they found themselves a rarity among thousands of eligible, single men, all eager for female flesh. In any event, I would come to identify myself with the other students in this class for the first months of my Bethel stay, because this group became a fraternity for us.

Anyway, the teachers began the class by giving instructions on how to be a good Bethelite. These instructions were mostly in the form of an exclusive super secret Bethel family book called *Dwelling Together in Unity*. This book looked and read like it was written in the early 1950s, which I found out later it actually was. It gave all kinds of important information that one could not possibly know on one's own, like how not to smell bad by taking showers and using deodorant. When you read through this book, you realized The Society was no longer going to attempt to control you through your congregation by putting pressure on your elders who then put pressure on your parents who in turn put pressure on you. Nope. Those days were over. Now they were going to control you <u>directly</u> with no middlemen. I kid you not; they would even tell you how you should perform personal bathroom habits.

Mull over <u>that</u> one for a minute.

Of course, at that time in my journey to find where God lives, I was a good Jehovah's Witness lemming. I just took it all in, eager to please. I was determined to be the best Bethelite in the whole wide world. You see, Jehovah's Witnesses often call their religion a "spiritual paradise," so I naturally thought that since Bethel was its hub, it had to be the place where this would be fulfilled more completely. I certainly didn't find it in my congregation back home. Of course, I was going to take full advantage of this "paradise" and toe the line like nobody's business because I so wanted it to work for me. I thought this spiritual paradise would be the next best thing to heaven that you could have on Earth, with everyone loving each other, everyone protecting each other and everyone bringing out the best in each other. A journey to God's House was not just about a physical location then, it really had to be a spiritual place as well. I figured whatever adjustments or sacrifices I had to make was a small price to pay to get to this spiritual paradise, this place where God lives. Most of the new guys with me felt the same way.

As it turns out, one of the guys in my group was a large, blubbery, obnoxious guy I'll call Big Tex. It wasn't that Big Tex was from Texas, maybe he was, and maybe he wasn't. It's just that to me he looked like he was from Texas due to the fact that a lot of what I knew in life up until then I had learned from watching cartoons. In these cartoons, Texans always wore big hats, drove big cars, had big guns, and spoke with big booming voices. This guy was big, loud, and wore cowboy boots. So you see, he just had to be from Texas. He sort of gave the appearance of a cross between Big Bird and Yosemite Sam without the mustache. During the class, Bethel instructors made him take off a baseball cap he often wore although he put it back on as soon as he could. They gave him "counsel" about not wearing the boots he wore, which he promptly ignored and kept wearing anyway. (I always imagined he'd put spurs on them if he could.) While all of us were dutifully listening to the instructors and doing our lessons, Big Tex was drawing naked women and other doodles in his book.

Big Tex displayed what I would soon learn Bethelites described as a "B.A." which was short for "bad attitude." I couldn't believe this guy. He didn't seem to want to be here. Didn't he <u>know</u> he was in God's House? Didn't he understand what a <u>privilege</u> it was to be here? At my first opportunity, I felt I <u>had</u> to talk to him to get his story. I did this even though he pretty much ignored the rest of us and wasn't all that friendly. Here's how the conversation went:

Me: Hey Big. How's it going?

Big Tex: 'k.

Me: What are you drawing?

Big Tex: [sarcastically] What's it look like?

Me: Uh... You OK? I mean... you don't really seem... well... like you want to be here.

Big Tex: Nope.

Me: Really? You don't want to be at Bethel?

Big Tex: Nope. Hate this place.

Me: [genuinely shocked] What? Why'd you come here?

Big Tex: Mom made me. Said I couldn't have my car back unless I put in at least a year. Dad said whatever mom said.

Me: Uhh...

Big Tex: Now that I see this place, I don't think I'll make it.

Me: Uhh...

Big Tex: Go away.

Me: Uhh...

True to his suspicion, Big Tex lasted all of a month before his journey ended. His housekeeper found stolen items in his room. I forget what exactly. When they searched the room more thoroughly to see if he stole anything else, they found a gun, a huge knife, and some girlie magazines. These things were all big no-no's at Bethel.

I'm not claiming this to be true, but I always imagined that this was what Big Tex said when he was booted out of Bethel: **YEEEEEEEEEHAAAAAAAAWWWW!**

Let 'em squirm

I was in class near the end of my first week at God's House and I heard several people talking.

They were discussing the issue of a Bethelite who never showed up. Those of us who were new heard about this the first day of our class. It seems that another new guy didn't show up like we did to say "here" when roll was called. Since we all considered it such a privilege to get asked to come to Bethel, we couldn't imagine what possibly could have happened to him. After all, even Big Tex came when he was supposed to. What was this guy's problem?

Well, we figured at first that perhaps he got sick or maybe his flight had been cancelled. We didn't think much of it that first day. But, by the end of the first week, people kept asking about this new missing Bethelite. By asking around, it seemed the new Bethelite was from the same region of the same state I was from. Hmmm. That was interesting. I knew many of the JWs in my neck of the woods because at one point, before I got my Witness act together, I was known for my parties and I knew many JWs that way. But, I never heard of this guy. Sure, I didn't know everybody. Still, I thought his name should have at least rang a bell.

In order to give you an idea of how I knew so many JW kids, I have a side story to tell you. I once had a party where I asked JWs to join us at a public place. It was the kind of place that I won't mention here as it might give away my identity. The thing was, I set up this party during a District Assembly. In our state, this assembly had thousands of JWs with many young people looking for fun on a Saturday evening. Well, by the time word got out, we had well over 300 Jehovah's Witness teenagers in this public place, at night, with boom boxes, dancing, bonfires, booze, and you name it. I remember this party was at its peak when we all seemed to dance as one big mob to *Shake It Up* by The Cars. The size and scope of this party was simply unheard of in typical JW circles because most JW parties were smallish, relatively quiet, and mostly boring. You know, buttoned up *Little House on the Prairie* type parties.

Unfortunately, some idiot, whom I didn't invite, started lighting off fireworks to get attention for himself. This in turn brought the wrong kind of attention for us all: the cops. So, when the Boys in Blue arrived, they got out their bullhorn and asked who was responsible for the mob. My name was being chanted by 300 JW kids: "Brock! Brock! Brock!" So, I was forced to make my way up to the multiple police cruisers blinding lights shining on us, my arms raised so I wouldn't be shot, apologizing for the mess. I told them simply, "The party got bigger than I expected," which was true. They said they wouldn't arrest me if I broke up the party then and there. Since they were not exactly happy with the noise, the illegal fires, the public drinking and the illegal fireworks, this request seemed reasonable to me. I asked for their bullhorn and used it to yell out to the crowd the classic line, "You guys don't have to go home, but you can't stay here!"

I heard later at least five more parties formed that night from the one I started and then broke up.

But I digress...

Getting back to the Bethel story, the next week we all continued to question the Bethel teachers about the mystery of the missing Bethelite, feigning concern about him. Actually, we just wanted to hear the dirt on this guy because it was interesting that somebody wouldn't show up to an assignment at God's House. Finally, somebody who worked at the Bethel offices relayed to us the answer we were looking for. They said, "This Bethelite did in fact make it to New York, but unfortunately he was left at the airport when somebody who was supposed to pick him up didn't. It seems we had a mix up and we neglected to pick up this brother."

They added, "We figure that he must have got back on another plane and went home." They continued, "He is not communicating with the Bethel offices any longer, so we are not sure of anything more than that." They finished by saying, "This situation is a shame."

Wow. I was shocked to hear this! That was _my_ experience they were talking about, not this other person's. I knew at that moment that there was some other JW who lived in the same general area as I lived who hadn't shown up for reasons unknown. Since the guy they were talking about was from my home state, they must have confused him with me. I was the poor slob left at the airport, not this other mystery man. I don't know what this other guy's problem was or why he didn't show up, but I knew that I hadn't turned around and gone home.

I almost blurted out, "Hey. No. That's not what happened!" to correct them and reveal to them that it was actually me who had been left at the airport. Then I thought better about it and said nothing. You see, I had told nobody about being left at the airport, because it was kind of humiliating. I was the only person who knew it happened to me.

I had been hoping all along that the Bethel powers that be would at least feel bad about leaving me. All the new Bethelites in my class who just now learned of this event thought it was a terrible thing to do to somebody - just leaving them like that stranded at the airport. I perceived that it put the Bethel offices in a bad light in front of the new guys.

I realized then too that the Bethel offices were at least aware that somebody screwed up and that the people responsible for abandoning me on that day were finally feeling the heat about it, even if for the wrong person. So, I said nothing.

I figured, let 'em squirm.

Hey, let's welcome the new guy by maiming him!

Newly arrived at God's House and a bit frightened since I never lived away from my home before, I was assigned to work in the factory making Bible literature. I was told this was a great privilege because this was what Bethel was all about. Everything else at Bethel centered around this effort, so being directly involved in making Bibles, books, magazines and pamphlets was integral to the work God needs here on Earth so that people all around the world could be saved by reading this material. This was truly holy work that I was blessed with being able to do.

My duties were mundane and it took great effort to get used to them. I was also getting used to the food, all the walking, New York City, the local culture, plus the intense schedule all Bethelites were under. I remember passing out exhausted every night during my first few weeks there. Even though they fed me well, I was always hungry. I actually lost weight at first, that is, until I could accustom myself to all the activity.

The early 1980s was a golden age for bodybuilding. Arnold Schwarzenegger (*Conan the Barbarian*) and Lou Ferrigno (*The Incredible Hulk*) were household names for many young guys like us who admired them. On top of everything else I did physically, I had a pretty faithful workout routine too, and I was a pretty good size myself with pretty big arms and chest and so on. Of course, I was nowhere near the size of those real bodybuilders. There were, however, some monster-sized dudes at Bethel at that time. The biggest guy of all was actually a real nice person whom I would later befriend. But as it turns out, it was the not-so-big guys there who had something to prove.

One day, I was taking a break among the boxes on the factory floor. It was late in the day and I was tired. I was reading my Bible because we had to read it through, cover to cover, within the first year at Bethel. I didn't know many people at Bethel then, as I was still new, so I was alone at that time. Well, four of the guys I recognized from my locker room approached me. They were laughing and joking with each other when they started talking to me. At first, it was small talk like, "Where you from?" and "Why'd you come here?" etc. Something told me they were not there to just chit chat with me because they had pretty much ignored me the first week. Besides, they were even now kind of standing away from me. Something felt wrong.

Then, the conversation took this ominous turn:

Dude #1: [muscular black guy in a ripped T-shirt] So, you work out?

Me: Yeah.

Dude #2: [tall lanky black guy in big thick glasses] How much you bench?

Me: Oh, over 290. Pushing for 300 now. I can reverse bench 250.

Dude #3: [little ugly brown guy with buckteeth] No way. You lie. Prove it.

Me: OK. Come to the gym with me this weekend and we'll see. Let's see what you bench.

Dude #4: [medium sized white guy] Well, we could all get a workout right here if we want to, right boys? [Grinning an evil grin]

Dude #1: Yeah, how about we do some "power lifts" guys? Hee hee.

Dude #2: Yeah. Hee hee. "Power lifts."

Dude #3: Sounds good!

Me: What? Power lifts?

Dude #1: Yeah, you see, we like to 'nitiate the new guys here by "power lifting" them into that trash bin over there! [he nodded at the huge trash container in the corner]

All dudes: HaHaHaHa. Yeah. Power lifting! Hee hee. Let's do it!

Me: Whaa?

Dude #2: Yes. You didn't hear about our initiations? You haven't been initiated yet. To be one of "us," you gonna get dumped.

Me: What? You're going to drop me into that six foot tall bin over there? It's empty. I could get hurt.

Dude #3: Oh well, twist like a cat.. make sure you land on your feet... [stupid looking buck-toothed grin]

Me: [incredulous] Gulp.

Now all four of them start coming closer to me, all of them with an evil look in their eyes, chuckling.

Me: [trying to barter with them, backing up] Look guys. I'm here at God's House doing His work. You shouldn't be hazing brothers like this. This isn't right...

They move closer to me, looking more menacing.

Me: [changing from scared to angry, flight mode to fight mode - full on] OK, here's the deal assholes! I have no doubt the four of you together can probably over power me and maybe get me into that trash can, but I swear to you this: the first one of you that touches me is going to get my full fury. I'll break his freaking face wide open, break his arm if I have to. The other three of you will have to pry me off that guy and have to get his eyeballs back from

46

my hands. [wild eyed, probably looking a bit crazy right now, huffing and puffing]

They all stop. They stop smiling too. They look at each other.

Me: [seething] Well, who's it gonna be?

All dudes: [in no particular order] Aw man, we're just joking. Yeah, dude, chill. Hey boy, you're all right. Ha Ha, man were you mad! Ooh, this boy's an animal. Whooie, I like this guy!

...and so on.

They slapped my back, told me I was "one bad boy", and welcomed me to Bethel.

Nice place.

I don't know to this day if they really were going to do that to me or not. I had heard about hazing before I got there, but somehow had never imagined I would be a victim. I guess because I was a little on the buff side and people generally didn't mess with me, it didn't seem possible.

All I know is that I had never been menaced like that before in my life and never have been again. Only in God's House had I been treated in such a way, and in my first days there on top of it. I would learn later that hazing was a long time Bethel tradition, done in many ways, some done benignly and other times done very dangerously.

I hate that memory, even to this day. And even though later I became sort of friends with these guys (I'm not sure why, self-preservation I guess) I never forgot what they did. I never looked at Bethel in the same way again either. It was a shame, as they took my innocence away from me in my first days at Bethel. I had looked forward to being in what JWs call a "spiritual paradise," that is, a place of refreshing comfort for all true Christians, where I thought the older guys would be big brothers to me.

Instead, I just learned to be on the lookout for more jerks like this while living there.

As it turned out, I would find them all too often.

Much ado about whiskers

In the 1960s and 1970s, long hair, beards, and mustaches were all the rage for most worldly people. The Jehovah's Witnesses took this time to be especially different from them by making sure to remain as clean cut as possible, as if they were still living in the 1950s. The Governing Body themselves had a special aversion to facial hair. To them, having it reeked of rebellion. That hasn't seemed to change even to this day. Well, in the early 1980s when I was headed for Bethel, this attitude about facial hair was still going strong, maybe stronger than ever. While non-JWs wore dramatic hairdos like the Mullet, Mohawk or Afro, and had facial hair sculpting, like the goatee or mutton chops, this only made the JW leaders dig in with their restrictions on facial hair all the more. This kind of facial hair would not be tolerated for those that practiced and lived in The Truth.

My congregation elders gave me "counsel" to shave my mustache because they had heard that Bethelites did not have them. They guessed it was so that Bethelites would be extra clean cut at God's House, over and above even other JWs. I had a mustache ever since I could grow one. Being young and vain, it was fairly traumatic to shave it, but shave it I did. It seemed weird to me right away that I could be a part-time pioneer (by putting in sixty hours a month preaching) in my own congregation, and still be able to have a mustache, yet not be allowed to keep it when I became a Bethelite.

Oh well. I did as I was told. Oops, I meant to say that I did as I was "counseled." You see, when elders "counseled" you, they were not "telling" you what to do. They wanted to give the illusion of being nice and of giving you a choice. They always said it was up to you, as what they gave you was just "counsel." But of course, if you did not take their "counsel" there would be repercussions, so you always did what they "counseled" if you knew what was good for you.

When I got to Bethel, I noticed right away that <u>lots</u> of guys had mustaches. Huh? What gives? One brother even looked to me like he kept a very low shaven beard. I was perplexed. I eventually got the nerve up to ask one of the Bethel Elders I knew about this issue. (A Bethel Elder was not just a regular elder in his congregation, he was an elder in the House of God too, a special kind of elder with an inside to the Bethel life and responsibilities there as well.) So, I figured asking him would be the best thing, since it was about "Bethel stuff." Regular elders didn't have a clue about "Bethel stuff." Well, what this Bethel Elder told me puzzled me then, and still does to this day.

He told me that Latino and black brothers were allowed to have mustaches at Bethel because it was "their culture." Since it was "cultural" for these dark-skinned brothers to have mustaches back at their home congregations, then it was OK for them to keep their facial hair in Bethel too. Of course, the white brothers had to shave theirs as there was no such "culture" of facial hair for these guys. Also, he added that the black brother I pointed out who wore a beard, well, that wasn't really a beard after all. You see, it was just that he got really bad bumps and acne for shaving close to his kinky-haired face. Because of this, he was allowed to grow his beard out "temporarily" so that his bumps and acne would go away. After that, he would be required to shave it as all good Witnesses did. So, no, I was told, it was not really a beard he was wearing, it was a "temporary grow-out" for medical reasons.

Hmmm.

At the time of being told these things, my mind just reeled and I didn't have anything to say. I was caught off guard by this strange reasoning. I became friends with the black brother with the beard later on, and I will state here for the record that he rarely shaved it since it took so long for his acne to clear up once he had problems with it. He only did shave from time to time to placate the elders once his face cleared up. When he did shave, the poor guy would get bumps and acne all over again. This was because his facial hair would grow into his skin if it were cut too close to the skin; his hair was so curly it just did that.

Sheesh.

To make this poor guy go through this all the time seemed silly to me. I asked myself wasn't that nature just showing everyone that this poor brother shouldn't shave at all, ever? Why make him grow it out once his acne cleared up, just to have him get more acne all over again later? Today, thinking about this just irritates me. Jehovah's Witnesses are often so stuck on their silly rules, they leave out common sense like this all the time. This was a good example of that kind of nonsensical rule enforcement that was completely unloving to this poor brother, making him suffer needlessly.

I never heard of such a thing before. I was incredulous about the Latino-or-black-mustache-is-OK explanation regarding "cultural acceptance." I don't recall exactly how my ensuing conversation with this elder went, but I do remember the plethora of questions I had for him about the subject after I got a chance to think about it. I'll summarize the questions I had for him here, but keep in mind that they were not necessarily in this order. Also, keep in mind that this was a discussion, not a series of questions I posed.

Jehovah's Witnesses are absolutely ruled by rules, especially at Bethel. Therefore, it just makes sense to want to have the rules made clear, doesn't it? Well, that's what I was trying to get, clarity.

I'll put these questions in bullet form for easy digestion:

- Isn't it racist to treat brothers differently, simply based on the color of their skin, even regarding facial hair?

- What if you simply <u>looked</u> Latino or black, but really were not. Was it OK to have a mustache then?

- What if you were mixed race, half white and half black for example? Could you grow a small mustache? Half a mustache?

- Who determines what is "cultural" for which ethnic groups, and where does this cultural difference acceptability end?

- For example, isn't it "cultural" for Hawaiian brothers to wear big floral shirts with no ties out in the preaching work in Hawaii? Could they then not have to wear suits like we do should they come to Bethel in New York?

- For that matter, isn't it "cultural" for some societies to allow their women to go topless? Then would it be OK for those women to go topless when they came to Bethel?

- Why is this mustache rule only at Bethel and not my home congregation? We had a mixed raced congregation there, so shouldn't Christian standards be the same everywhere?

The knowledgeable Bethel Elder didn't like these questions. He pretty much told me that was the way it was, and that I shouldn't be such a wise acre. A bit annoyed, he left me.

His brush off of my questions just made me think about this subject all the more. After all, when I didn't get answers, I didn't have closure. It got me to thinking about the entire facial hair issue to begin with which Jehovah's Witnesses make such a big deal about. I just had to have a follow-up conversation with this same Bethel Elder again about this subject in more detail.

Here are some highlights of my follow-up questions to him:

- Why is it wrong for any Christian to wear a mustache or beard for that matter? Didn't God make it grow on our faces?

Doesn't God <u>want</u> men to have beards and mustaches? What's next, no eyebrows?

- How does shaving or not shaving the God-given hair on my face reflect my faith in any way? Does Jehovah really love me less because I wear facial hair that He caused to grow on my face in the first place?

- If the argument that we don't have beards is because they are not accepted in a "business setting" (this is what JWs argue by the way) then why could I point out many CEOs and other executives from Fortune 500 companies who have beards? Wouldn't the business world know if beards were acceptable better than a JW at Bethel? How do these business guys with beards flourish if it is so objectionable to have them?

- If the argument that we don't have beards is because they are not accepted in a "business setting," then why would that even matter at all to a JW? Isn't the business world in general worldly, so why care what the world thinks about us?

- Ancient Jews of the Bible set themselves apart by their appearance. Couldn't we as JWs all do that by all of us simply growing our beards out to show ourselves "not part of the world"?

- Did The Society really think we would be less objectionable and less of a pariah in the world's eyes, so we would be listened to in our preaching work just by having clean-shaven faces?

The Bethel Elder simply stopped trying to answer my questions and walked away shaking his head. He muttered under his breath that I was being ridiculous. I suppose a not-formally-written, but otherwise enforced Bethel "rule" that allows black brothers to do one thing while disallowing the same thing to white brothers is not ridiculous?

I have brought this up in many ways, many times, both in and out of Bethel over the years to many Jehovah's Witness elders, but this particular discussion seems to always end the same way with them: deaf ears. After all, it seems much easier for them to take the JW "much ado about whiskers" stance than to just leave people alone about this very personal issue.

By the way, can you guess what I'm wearing on my face right now while I am writing this story?

It's great to be The King!

The early 1980s was a time of many good movies. When I was in Bethel in those years, Mel Brooks released a wonderfully funny movie called *History of the World: Part I*. There was a classic line in this movie that was repeated over and over again: "It's good to be the King." This was used when the king got to do anything he wanted, like eat all the food at a banquet, or grab any woman anywhere he wanted to any time he wanted to. My friends and I used to say this line to each other all the time, cracking ourselves up with it. We used to quote lines from *Monty Python and the Holy Grail* too, which was another Bethel favorite. If for example, we cut ourselves with something at work, we'd say, "Oh, it's just a flesh wound," in a silly Monty Python-like voice. If you don't know what any of these lines mean, or don't know what the heck I'm talking about, then you're probably very young. You might want to do an online search and you should find a video clip of these scenes. Better yet, watch these movies; they're classics.

Anyway, my "table head" at that time was Writing Committee Elder GS-. For those of you who don't know what table head means, each Bethelite was assigned a particular table to sit at for breakfast and dinner (aka lunch). We were required to eat at the assigned table for those two meals. We could eat anywhere we wanted to for the evening meal (that we called supper) as well as all of the weekend meals. Because we sat at the same table each week day for the first two meals of the day, The Society made sure that each table had what they deemed an appropriate table head, usually a Bethel Elder and an appropriate "table foot," usually an up and comer who would one day be a Bethel Elder if he was not already. The table head and table foot were usually married, but didn't have to be. If you were a single table head or table foot, you were probably a long time prominent Bethelite. The other seats were filled with a variety of Bethel peons like me.

The table head was yet another authority figure you had at Bethel and they had a measure of influence on your Bethel life. Since you ate most of your formal meals with these folks, you certainly did not want to have anything but a good relationship with them. It didn't hurt to get along with the others at the table too. Now as I mentioned earlier, GS- was on the Writing Committee, and that standing was no small potatoes, even though he was not a member of the Governing Body (GB). At that time, you could only be a GB member if you were one of the 144,000 going to heaven. Jehovah's Witnesses think only 144,000 people are going to heaven, the rest get the consolation prize of life on Earth... if they are fortunate and don't tick off God too much. Only these 144,000 "anointed" people could be GB. By the way, to be a GB you had to be male as well. Females could not be GB, and could not be elders and basically could not be a whole lot of things in the JW religion. But at Bethel, the ladies at least made good housekeepers (aka cleaning ladies).

At the time, I thought it was cool having GS- for my table head. After all, this guy helped write the *Watchtower!* This is the key JW magazine that leads the way for all JW doctrine to be disseminated throughout the world for the millions of Jehovah's Witnesses who practiced the faith. "Wow!" I thought, "Where does GS- get his ideas from to put into the *Watchtower?*... Wait," I thought. "Didn't God only speak to the 144,000? Why did they need this person? How does this work? When God talks to the Governing Body, do they channel it to GS- who furiously scribbles it down, like a holy stenographer? What about all the other 144,000, who don't live at Bethel? After all, aren't they 'anointed' too? So, how do all of these people communicate to GS- what to write in the *Watchtower?*"

I had many questions like these, but I never did get up the nerve to ask him because I was always afraid I might ruin our otherwise good relationship with a question he deemed inappropriate. You see, JWs in leadership positions do not like it when other JWs ask questions that show that they think for themselves. This kind of independent thinking is looked down on in all JW circles, and Bethel certainly wasn't the place for it.

One day, Brother GS- asked those of us at the table to relate what we learned from the weekly Bible reading. He often did that to keep the conversation positive and on a spiritual note. This week we had been reading chapters around Exodus 22. This particular reading was filled with Jewish laws. So, this made his question an extremely open-ended one, since there were so many laws in those chapters to comment on.

I don't recall who commented on what exactly. Most of those at the table took the predictable high road and performed the same old JW song and dance by saying something like this: "I like the law that said you couldn't charge interest if you loaned money to your brother. See, this just shows how loving Jehovah is." Another would say something like: "I think it is interesting that thieves had to pay back what they stole many-fold. You know, if we did that today, I believe all stealing would stop!" And around the table it went, with all sorts of various appropriate sound bites.

"Typical drivel," I was thinking. "There are way more interesting things in that reading than what these guys are saying." I was recalling a particular verse in Exodus 22:16, which states: "If a man seduces a virgin who is not betrothed and lies with her, he shall give the bride-price for her and make her his wife. If her father utterly refuses to give her to him, he shall pay money equal to the bride-price for virgins."

I noticed that GS- was looking at me and he seemed to know I had something to say, but was not saying it. Maybe it was by the look on my face, I don't know for sure. You see, this brother was a bit curious, and fairly reasonable. I think he wanted to hear something fresh from the newest kid at the table. So, he pressed me specifically:

GS-: Well Brock, what did you learn from the reading?

Me: Um... [hesitating at first, then getting bold] Well, I found the passage about the law regarding seducing a virgin interesting. You know, the guy who seduced the virgin had to pay the "bride price" for her if the dad found out about it and, um, as long as she wasn't married or engaged... uh...

[I stopped and was thinking to myself how to say it]

GS-: Yes, and...

Me: [I blurted out] So, basically, I learned that if you were an ancient Jew, fornication was OK as long as you could afford it!

Table: Gasp!

Well, the young guys at the table started laughing, and the pious table end couple started shaking their heads with disapproval. GS-'s wife was poking and whispering to her husband, obviously telling him, "Say something to this boy." GS- waited for the hubbub to die down a little while he smiled slyly at me. When it got quiet he simply said, "That's true."

GS- changed the subject and the table went on with more positive prattle, but he looked over at me with a wry smile, almost as if he knew what I was thinking. What I was thinking was, "Boy, in those days, it must have been great to be The King."

Of course, I never said it out loud.

My music is holier than your music

As my journey continued at God's House decades ago, I found that people there were in an album-burning frame of mind. Thanks to rumors about backwards masking and subliminal messages in popular music, this was a woeful time to be in Bethel if you were a music lover. You basically had to hide what you listened to.

It is amusing now thinking back on what was considered scandalous music in my day. I mean, this was the year Olivia Newton John sang the provocative *Physical* and the J. Geils Band sang the risqué *Centerfold*. Wow, some shocking music, huh? Compare that to today with Cee Lo Green's *F**k You* or 2 Live Crew's *Pop that P***y*, and you have to laugh about how innocent we actually were back then.

But the fact that our so-called risqué music was in reality quite innocent in retrospect didn't stop the pious in my day from condemning what we listened to. Here's a recreated conversation I had with a brother at Bethel about this subject. He was a ministerial servant in his congregation (again, think elder in training). He was not a particularly important person at Bethel, but he did have the typical outlook of many Bethelites and other Witnesses at that time. He also was a long time Bethelite given to bossing us newer ones around.

Him: [friendly-like and smiling] Hey, I noticed you like Elton John because you have some of his albums. Haven't you seen our Bethel list of "music that debases"? We're throwing away all our albums on this list, you know.

Me: [puzzled] Um, no, sorry. I read the *Watchtower* article on "music that debases," but I didn't know there was an actual "list."

Him: Yes. Here. [he gives me a faded looking, one hundred times re-photo copied piece of paper which was half typed and half hand scribbled. The list contained dozens of album names on it that were added to manually after somebody typed them in, then some of them were crossed out.]

Me: [trying to take the list in] Uhhhh, I heard some Led Zeppelin albums are being thrown out because of the backwards masking in its songs that supposedly says "worship Satan" or something like that. I haven't personally heard any backward masking myself though, that is, to verify this is actually true... Um, so, what's wrong with Elton John music?

Him: [matter of fact-like] Well, he's gay. I thought everybody knew that.

Me: [puzzled] Yes, I heard he said he was bisexual recently. But his life is actually kind of a mystery isn't it? I mean, we don't really know who he is romantic with. He's kind of closed mouthed about that though isn't he? I mean, I really don't know much about him personally in any other way. So, why does that make his <u>music</u> wrong to listen to?

Him: [sarcastically] Duh. He promotes the gay lifestyle which is contrary to the Christian lifestyle. That's why his albums are on the "list" of music that debases Christians, and why we should throw them out if we own them.

Me: [thinking out loud] Hmmm. Well, I don't know if I would say that being gay by itself is <u>promoting</u> the lifestyle. I mean, his music never says anything about homosexuality at all, let alone promote it. And, like I said, he doesn't talk about it much except for maybe that one article in *Rolling Stones* magazine as far as I know. Can you give me an example of a <u>song</u> he has put out that promotes the gay lifestyle? Specifically, in the albums I own?

Him: [now indignant] Look, it doesn't matter. If Elton John is gay, then his music is based on the gay perspective. Period. Christians shouldn't listen to it. We should not be supporting the gay lifestyle by purchasing a gay person's music, see?

Me: [pushing back] Well, <u>you</u> like the Rolling Stones and Van Halen. Those guys are notorious heterosexual fornicators, serial fornicators in fact, and they lead very decadent lifestyles of sex and drugs and so forth. Not only are they well known for this lifestyle, they actually <u>do</u> promote it in their music. So, by your logic, Christians should not listen to them either because you would be supporting <u>that</u> lifestyle, right?

Him: Ummm...

Me: In fact, thinking about it, there is more of a case against those guys, as their actual music itself sings about things like *Running with the Devil* and *Sympathy for the Devil* not to mention *Hot for teacher* and *Let's spend the night together*. <u>That</u> my friend is promoting immorality and sin.

Him: Ummm... Well... Yes, but...

Me: [now on a roll] To go further, according to your theory, a Christian should not listen to any song by, watch a movie with an actor in, read a book written by or watch a game with a professional athlete in it that has anybody known for fornication, lying, greediness, thievery, drunkenness or drug abuse. If you do, you are then "paying for" <u>their</u> lifestyles too. I've never seen a place in the Bible that ranks homosexuality as being somehow a worse sin than any of those sins, have you?

Him: Uh... No.

Me: OK. So are you agreeing with me that homosexuality is not a worse sin in God's eyes than say, heterosexual immorality?

Him: Yes. Sure.

Me: Right. They are all referred to as "serious sin" and all are against the Christian lifestyle, right?

Him: Yes... But...

Me: Sorry, no "but." When you stop supporting all these worldly people who promote <u>their</u> immoral lifestyles in their art and activities, I'll throw away my Elton John albums. Deal?

Him: [self righteous throat clearing] Humph... Well.. Whatever... You can do as you like.

Me: OK. Well, it sounds like we both will be doing what we like then. [giving the list back to him] Talk to you later.

Fast forward to today: My taste in music has changed many times since those days and I really don't listen to Elton John's music all that much anymore.

But it's not because some bossy, hypocritical, self-appointed music fascist told me I shouldn't.

Epic breasts

Early on in my journey to find where God lives, I had promised myself I would <u>not</u> be one of those people whose journey would end prematurely by being kicked out of Bethel. It turned out that getting ousted was not all that uncommon. The bar for getting kicked out of Bethel was much lower than the bar for getting disfellowshipped, because the standard for the behavior of a Bethelite was set so high. As a result, getting ousted was actually relatively easy to do.

I saw guys get kicked out for fighting, kicked out for being lazy and not working, kicked out for hurting themselves and then not being <u>able</u> to work. They got kicked out because they ticked off the wrong guy who had political power, and they got asked to leave if they just generally had a "bad attitude." I knew of guys who got kicked out for flirting with somebody's wife, for stealing, for listening to too much "devil influenced" music, for looking at porn, for calling in sick too much, for bringing in a weapon, and for being engaged and then not getting married. You could be asked to leave Bethel for so many reasons, it almost seemed to me they made up new offenses on a weekly basis to give people the boot.

But, by far the biggest reason for getting kicked out of Bethel was for immorality. Sometimes it was gay immorality, but usually it was just plain heterosexual encounters with single girls that did them in. It didn't even have to be for fornication itself. You could get kicked out for just "fooling around" with a girl (petting). You see, there we were, young men at our sexual peak, basically walking boners, and we had better not do <u>anything</u> about it. Even masturbation was forbidden. No quarter was given for that kind of behavior from us horny little bastards. One mistake and we were gone!

Well, I actually spent most of my young life up until that time getting into trouble with girls, over and over again, from as far back as puberty. Heck, maybe even before that. At one point in high school, my parents were too busy to go to Witness meetings at the Kingdom Hall and we became what JWs call "inactive." It was then that I had the time of my life with worldly girls who didn't have qualms about having sex like Witness girls did. So I had lots of it with them. I wasn't baptized at the time either, and that meant I couldn't be DF'd. You see, you can only be disfellowshipped if you are baptized as a Jehovah's Witness. Still, not being baptized as an adult in the JW faith meant I was going to die at Armageddon for sure (or so every Witness believed) so that wasn't really a viable alternative in the long run either, that is, to avoid baptism to avoid disfellowshipping. Avoiding baptism when you "knew better" was simply sealing your doom. So my quandary was this: do I get baptized and possibly DF'd for my bad behavior and thus get ostracized for that, or do I avoid getting baptized to avoid getting DF'd and thus get ostracized for not committing to the faith?

I eventually was "saved" from that problem and all of that sexual misconduct by a cool, caring brother who hunted me down and told me I was in danger of losing my everlasting life. This guy even stalked me at my work and watched me in secret. He would then chide me when I spoke to worldly girls at work and tell me how I was walking on thin ice with God. He said we all needed to practice sexual self-regulation. He said a "real man" would do that and not give in to sexual sin. Eventually, with this cool brother's help, I finally "got hold of myself." I was even brave enough to get baptized once I thought I had this sexual purity thing mastered. Hooray! Now I was saved!

Well, maybe not. You see, there was always that sex thing getting in my way. Even though I was now baptized, that only meant I only could be saved. Jehovah's Witnesses believe it is not only possible, but likely, to be in a saved position, but to lose it by bad conduct and thus be destroyed forever even after expressing your faith in Jesus and so on. So, if I gave in to the sex sin again, well, that meant I was going to die at Armageddon regardless.

(Amusing side note: The "cool" brother who got me back on track into the JW religion and who pushed me to get baptized, later cheated on his wife, who promptly divorced him. He eventually left the JW faith as a result of his ensuing miserable single life of "no sex." Oh well, so much for "being a man," sexual self-regulation, and not being destroyed at Armageddon. Maybe I should have returned the favor and stalked him at his work to keep him in line?)

Anyway, I tried over and over again to be good about this sex thing. I didn't want to die at Armageddon, but my penis was getting in the way of that hope. That dang appendage was going to be the end of me yet. So, renewing my vow of chastity, I buckled down and pioneered and did all the right Witness things. I did it long enough to apply for and get into Bethel. I thought that would save me. After all, I would be in God's House where all the men there would be my big brothers who would understand my plight. Certainly they would be eager to help me out, patiently understanding my struggle, right?

Yeah, right.

Anyway, once I was at Bethel, I came to realize that I was on my own. Worse, there was a war afoot that I hadn't anticipated fighting. You've heard of Germ Warfare, Chemical, or Nuclear Warfare? Well, that stuff is for sissies. In our minds, we fought the hardest fight of all: Sexual Warfare. Yes, we were sure that some "sisters" (JW females) waged this because they themselves figured out that if they had sex with a horny Bethelite, it would be a straight ticket to marriageville with a "good brother." Also, better yet, once he confessed to the sex, he would probably get kicked out of Bethel. Thus, you both could then start your marriage and new life together away from that dratted

65

institution. Smart sisters, they. "Foul temptresses," "Evil daughters of Eve," we thought.

(Note to non-JWs: As I mentioned before, we all called each other "brother" and "sister," sort of like the Amish do. This actually sounded kind of strange when you said a sentence like this: "I really think that sister is hot." By the way, if people actually were brothers in that they had the same parents, then we described them as "fleshly brothers.")

As it was, it seemed that some guys were clueless about this sexual warfare being waged by those vixen-like sisters. If these guys <u>did</u> know about it, then they just didn't care and suffered the consequences. Others like me were scared of this situation. Having sex wasn't new to us, but we just didn't want to leave Bethel in humiliation. Besides, that certainly was no way to start a relationship. Therefore, we were very careful.

Well, in my congregation there were a couple of sisters who were actual fleshly sisters with whom I came to be friends. I flirted with them, but I never gave it a thought to date or get too close to either of them because that would basically be like crapping where I ate. Since these girls were in my Bethel-assigned local congregation, any stuff between us that didn't work out would only lead to many months of misery. Better to maybe mess up with other girls, but not ones right there in my face every week in my congregation.

Unfortunately, one of these girls happened to have the one thing that was very important to me back in those days: she had breasts that could only be described as **EPIC**.

Let's call her Sister Mary Mamms. Now Mary was a nice girl and cute enough, though not beautiful. But then again, who cared about that? After all, she had those epic breasts. When we spoke alone in the congregation, we were never really alone, there was me, Mary, and her boobs, who were always butting in on the conversation; I tell you, those breasts were rude. They also seemed to be trying to jump out of her blouse. Mary covered them up properly as a nice Witness girl should, but being epic, they had a mind of their own.

Those breasts were always talking to me too: "Hello there big boy. We're here! Look at us you nasty little man. Let us out! Come and play with us!" and so on. Boy, I loved and hated those breasts.

Whenever Mary caught me looking at them, she always smiled. She knew what I was doing and I quickly pretended I wasn't doing what I was doing. We never really spoke about it, but it was a stupid game of chicken I was playing with Mary, and those breasts, and they all seemed to enjoy it.

One day, my roommate wanted to get to know her fleshly sister better. He asked me to arrange a "group" in order for us to get together for that. The group would be the two sisters (who were actual sisters), and him, and me. Now, you must understand that in Bethel one of the million rules we had to follow was that if you were alone in a room with a person of the opposite sex who was not your blood relative, you had to leave the door to your room open, that is, from the public hallway. This situation got weird for me one time when my roommate's grandmother came to visit him at Bethel. He was out for a little while when she arrived, so I let her in our room. There she sat on his bed, waiting for him to come back to the room, looking like a giant prune in a Jackie Kennedy outfit. Yet, I had to keep the door open to not give the impression that I could be doing improper things with grandma. Brilliant rule!

But I digress.

One way around this rule was if two guys were with two girls, then we could close the door because that was now a "group." So, we asked the girls in, closed the door, and we each eventually paired off and went to our own sides of the room. My friend had acquired a very big room in the Towers Building somehow (which was tough to do as a new Bethelite). I gladly moved in with him. Because the room was so big, we actually got to have some real alone time with these girls when we went to on our own sides of the room.

Well, my roommate was busy with the one sister, doing some intense flirting, and there I was with Sister Mary Mamms on my bed. I liked Mary well enough, but I didn't really want to do any fooling around with her, so I just planned on talking and flirting.

Mary changed the game, however. She started to tickle me. I tickled back. The tickling got more intense and we started thrashing around on the bed, giggling like crazy. Next thing I knew, BOOOOIIIINGGG! Her blouse actually flew open! There were her breasts in a very sheer see-through and skimpy bra, staring directly at me! They did in fact come out to play! I didn't do this to her blouse and neither did Mary. Those darn breasts did that on their own! Epic breasts are like that you know; they can't be controlled. Mary just opened her mouth in mock horror looking down at her wayward breasts.

I stared.

Time stood still.

I could hear my heart pounding, loud, and in slow motion...

Mary giggled, but made no move to close her blouse.

You know in the movies how they show someone's life passing before their eyes just before they die? They show flashes of a thousand scenes all at once and then the person dies? Well, that happened to me, except my Bethel life flashed before my eyes. After that, my future humiliation played out in my mind of me returning to my congregation as a horny sinner, with everyone scoffing and shaking their heads at me. Then Armageddon came. Then I was dead, my carcass rotting in the sun, turning to dust and blowing away. All of this in a few seconds.

I jumped up as if I was electrocuted and quickly said to her, "I'll let you get that." I went over to the others and started talking to them while Mary fiddled with her blouse. My roommate and Mary's sister didn't notice what happened. Whew! Thank goodness! I was safe.

The next time I saw Mary was at my Bethel-assigned local congregation where we both attended our meetings. After that day in my room, Mary never treated me the same way again. It wasn't that she was cruel to me, or that she did anything particularly mean to me at all. No, nothing like that. But she had definitely lost interest in me completely, that much was clear.

Personally, I think those epic breasts put her up to it.

Seniority, it's the only white meat

As a young man dropped in the middle of Bethel life, I found that most everything there was based upon seniority from doing what JWs call "full-time service years." Pioneering and missionary work was one way to get full-time service years. So was being a special "servant" like a Circuit or District Overseer. And of course, so was Bethel service. Your entire Bethel life was governed by this seniority, and the only way you could move up on the seniority ladder was to simply live longer while serving in one of these capacities. Of course, another way for you to get seniority was to wait for others to leave Bethel or simply die. Keep in mind though, that at any time, somebody new could come to Bethel with more service years than you, and get in line in front of you.

I grew up as a Jehovah's Witness, and I knew about the JW pecking order. At least I thought I did. At Bethel, the obsessive focus on full-time service years was entirely new to me. It proved to be a special bummer because I had none. You see, I didn't "full-time" pioneer before going to Bethel, I only "part time" pioneered, which meant I had exactly zero full-time service years when I got there. That meant, among the thousands of Bethelites there, I once again found myself at the bottom of the JW heap.

You don't think I might be making too much of this seniority thing do you? You wouldn't think that if you understood what that meant for us there.

For example, right off the bat my first months in Bethel, they put me into a four-man room. This meant living in a room with two sides to it, each side with two beds, but only one shared bathroom. That was clue #1 that I was not just the low man on the totem pole, I was the face on the pole that was buried under ground. Most rooms at Bethel were for two people, so most single people like me roomed with one other single person. If you were single and particularly important and had enough full-time service, you could get your own room. Being put into a four-man room was the worst, because it meant that four guys had to share one bathroom, each trying to get ready in the morning after the 6:30 AM bell rang. We had to be dressed and down for breakfast by 7:00 AM in time to hear our morning text. That also meant four times the noise in the room and four different personalities trying to get along in that room. This was not an apartment, mind you, it was a room!

I stayed in the old Towers Hotel that The Society bought and then converted the hotel rooms into Bethel residence quarters. So, we're not talking about a lot of space to begin with. Rooming together also meant my three other roommates bossed me around all the time because they were all older than I was, and had more "years." In order to get a better rooming situation, you could "bid" on rooms that opened up, but people with longer full-time service simply bid each year on the best rooms. This "room bidding" process simply meant the biggest dogs in Bethel got the best rooms. Always. It also meant guys like me got the dregs. I actually never bothered to bid on any room for my entire stay at Bethel since it was pointless for me to do so.

Another example of the importance of seniority arose when we were assigned to a local congregation to attend our five weekly meetings. "Local" proved to be a relative term, as most of us low seniority people got sent far away to congregations nowhere near Bethel. I had a forty minute subway ride to upper Manhattan which I thought was bad until I heard of other Bethelites who had to travel over an hour to get to their meetings, every week, for five meetings a week! The longer you were at Bethel, the better chance you had to be moved to a congregation that was more easily accessible. In fact, the very old timers at Bethel with all the power simply met at the "Bethel Kingdom Hall" right there on the premises with absolutely zero commute. People like that got many hours back for themselves each week for this reason alone, as they didn't spend time in a subway or car ride to get to their meetings.

People with the appropriate seniority could do other things, like order furniture to be made for them for only the cost of the materials. The skilled wood working Bethelites there could hand craft almost anything for you for cheap, that is if you had enough full-time service years. This was the case for other things like clothes, briefcases and anything else Bethel artisans could make for you. If you had the years, you had the goods. I found myself looking longingly at other people's furniture, as the junk they gave me was barely usable and distinctly ugly.

People with seniority could usually keep a car too, because they would be in line to get a coveted Bethel parking spot. Having a car in Bethel could be a good thing as it gave you total freedom, especially from the subways. Nevertheless, it was costly to own a car. If you were a peon with a car, you had to constantly move the car around on the street to keep up with street cleaning times and avoid being ticketed. So, you would always be hunting for open parking spots. People with seniority avoided the issue entirely as it gave them access to Bethel parking spots as well as the Bethel mechanics. I found out later that many who owned cars would offer rides to the meetings to others, as long as in return they gave those car owners their subway money. This extortion was said to "defray" the cost of the car, but of course they would have had the car anyway. These high seniority car owners knew there was always an underprivileged Bethelite glad to give up his subway money for a nice car ride to the meetings. This was an example of seniority meaning you had more money from leveraging your seniority options.

I found out too that when it came to haircuts, long time servants could get the schedule they wanted to see the barber or hairdresser. They could also get their hair cut the way they wanted and maybe even get services like perms, hair dying and so on. The rest of us were told when to get a haircut. We simply went down to the barber like sheep at our appointed date, and were subsequently shorn to the standards of Bethel, with zero input on how it would look. If we wanted it longer here or shorter there, too bad, those requests were usually ignored.

Seniority also had an impact on where you ate. That is, the dining room you ate in, the table itself in that dining room, and the position at the table. You see, some dining rooms were better than others for many reasons. First, you wanted to be in a dining room located in the Bethel residence building you lived in. This was usually the case, but not guaranteed. If you didn't eat and live in the same building, you had a much longer walk just getting to your meals each day. Also, the smaller the dining room, the better, because there was less noise and fussing going on in them. There was more of the desirable food per person in the smaller dining rooms as well. You also wanted a table nearest the exit for quick in and out, so some tables were more desirable than others were. Also, the head of the table and his wife were at the best position in the table, as they always got the main course part of the meal first and then passed the plate along to the rest at the table. If you were unfortunate enough to be at the wrong part of the table, well, you got the worst servings every time. For example, if Bethel had chicken that day, you didn't expect the juicy breasts to be there for you, you expected the necks or backs. Hopefully your table head was fair and passed "to the right" sometimes, and then changed it to passing "to the left" other times, in order to mitigate this problem. But that also was not guaranteed. Besides, to me it always seemed that the passing went against my best interests at the worst possible times, even if he did mix it up from time to time.

As a result of all these things, seniority had a strange impact on me regarding material things. You see, I grew up in a middle class environment, so I really didn't think about material things all that much up until then. My parents pretty much provided for me what I needed, and I came to realize they provided me fairly nice stuff, not "just get by" stuff. I lived in a house with few siblings, and we all ate well and had our own rooms with nice furnishings. If I didn't get something I wanted from my parents, then I simply worked a part time job and bought it. I never wanted for much.

In Bethel however, this completely changed. Due to this seniority issue and my always lacking what I wanted, as well as having to wait for certain things, or just not get what I wanted at all, I found myself for the first time in my life coveting other people's stuff. Wishing for more than what I had was new to me because what I had was pretty lousy. At Bethel, we were all forbidden from taking a part time worldly job, so making more money was not even an option. The Bethelites who had the "nice stuff" always seemed to find a way to show these things off, so I suffered envy for the first time in my young life for that reason as well.

By the end of my Bethel stay, I couldn't wait to get my own job to make my own money and just buy whatever darn thing I wanted, when I wanted. I really resented that I was given everything by the Bethel ruling class as if I were a child. I hated that I had very little say in what I got, and no real way to get the things I wanted, other than "put in a request" and then wait for the seniority thing to kick in. For me, it usually didn't.

It was ironic that after living in God's House I found myself actually wishing for more material things, as well as desiring position in life, more than I ever would have had I not gone there. You would think a religious institution would teach you to not be materialistic, but Bethel had the opposite effect on me. I no longer took for granted a nice car, a good desk, a good quality briefcase, my own room, and the best portions of food. For the first time in my life, I wanted nice things and lots of them. I also wanted "seniority" in life, that is, the pull to get what I wanted.

Bethel taught me to want all that.

Look, it got so bad there, I found myself just wishing for that juicy chicken breast I never seemed to get at the dinner table.

That was because at Bethel, seniority was the only white meat.

Watchman, Watchman, what of the long terrifying night?

As my journey continued in God's House in the early 1980s, while Mr. T had his first fight with Rocky and E.T. was phoning home, I was assigned my first "walking watchman duty." This was an assignment given to us young Bethelites above and beyond all our other assignments. Not all Bethelites got this duty. To me, this was essentially Bethel's version of jury duty, only much worse, more frequent, and you never got out of it.

Before I go on, I'd like to mention here that the *Watchtower* magazine itself took its name from Isaiah 21:11, that reads, "Watchman, Watchman, what of the night?" This scripture basically was said to imply that true Christians were to be like those watchmen of old who were responsible for warning people of impending danger. The watchman of course used a watchtower to do his job, so, the name of the main magazine of Jehovah's Witnesses was therefore called: *Watchtower*. (The other JW magazine called *Awake* has a much more mundane etymology. It's just called that because it was simply written to help people to "keep awake.")

Hence, Bethel service had what was called "watchman duty" which took this principle of being a watchman much more literally. Watchman duty in general had many forms and I cannot tell you about all of them. I can only tell you what I was assigned to do myself, which was the factory "walking watchman duty." Walking watchman was a specific kind of watchman duty which required you to walk around during your watch while making sure that the buildings were secure. You will soon see, however, that this duty involved much more than that. There evidently were other kinds of watchmen duties that did not require this walking around part of it, but I never had one of those cakewalk assignments.

The walking watchman duty was considered by many to be the worst of the watchman duties. This was especially so if you had it at the four factory buildings at 117 Adams Street rather than, say, a watchman duty at any of the Bethel residence buildings or at the smaller white collar office buildings. This time period was before The Society bought the large Sands Street or Pearl Street factory buildings. So when I say "the factory," I mean those buildings limited to the 117 Adams Street address as well as the three buildings connected to it via bridges over the streets of Brooklyn.

The mechanics of the walking watchman duty was like this: You hoofed it alone, outside in the dark and in the elements through the streets of Brooklyn, over to the 117 Adams Street property to check in at the front desk. I forget the exact time we were required to be there, but let's say it was around 9:00 PM on a weekday night. You were required to do this duty even though you worked that day, all day, and would work the next day as well.

After checking in, you would relieve the normal "day watchman," who before leaving would give you a flashlight, a map, a strange looking satchel with a keyhole in it, and a sheet of instructions. You would dutifully read those instructions, and after about an hour of sitting at the front desk staring at the clock, you would begin your "walking" part of the watchman duty. This consisted of going to pretty much every floor in all four buildings through a maze of stairs, elevators, and bridges. On each floor, and usually at both ends of each floor, you would find a key hanging on the wall in a particular spot as indicated on the map. You would take the key and stick it into the strange satchel machine, then turn it. This would later indicate to an auditor that you had in fact been at that spot at that time.

Now, this entire satchel and key business was set up to let you know that you could not fake the walking part of your watchman duty. The map was given you because there were so many keys to find, it wasn't assumed you would be able to remember them all even if you had done this duty many times. You were instructed quite specifically that you were <u>not</u> to miss turning any of those keys. If you didn't do your watchman duty correctly, then you'd have to do another watchman duty to make up for it.

So, you would find a key and then proceed to the next key according to the instructions and map that was given to you. Floor after floor, in the dark, with only your flashlight to guide you, all alone, you would go to find your keys. Trudge, trudge, hunt, search, crank, crank, climb, climb. Walk, walk, seek, seek, turn, turn, climb, climb. We would sometimes use the elevator to get to some floors, other times we would use the stairs. We would cross the many bridges that connected the buildings together over the streets of Brooklyn, over and back again, never going outside however, always staying inside the Bethel owned structures. We would do this over and over, until the last key was found and turned on the last floor of the last building. It wasn't always easy to find the keys, as sometimes they might not be in the location where they should be, or something might be blocking the location where the key was. If that was the case, well, too bad. You had to find that darned key or your watchman duty was in jeopardy.

Once you were done with your rounds, the map would lead you back to the main building and the main floor to where you started. There, you would wait for the early morning when another watchman would relieve you. You would slog back to your room in the wee hours of the morning through the streets of Brooklyn, again in the dark and alone, to try to get a few hours of sleep before you would hear the 6:30 AM bell ring. (Yes, Bethel had a "bell," just like in school, only remember that this was where you lived!) When that bell did ring, you were expected to get up to go to your regular job as usual. No quarter was given you just because you had this walking watchman duty the night before.

Exhausting.

Now if that wasn't bad enough, they always told the new walking watchman guy a bit of Bethel lore which I am still not sure to this day is true or not. I suppose they could have made it up to mess with us in order to make your watchman night even more disconcerting than it already was. I don't know for sure. This is what they told us before we started doing our walking watchman duty for the first time: "One day, a young Bethelite was on walking watchman duty in the factory, and he pressed the elevator door button. When the elevator door opened, he stepped into it, but actually only stepped into space, because the elevator door opened with no elevator in it! The Bethelite fell eight stories to his death! SPLAT!"

I guess the moral of the story was, "Stay alert, jackass!"

I'd like to put this all into perspective for you now. I was a young kid never having left home before. I traveled very far to a strange city and was still trying to get accustomed to navigating the fears of that city, what with the muggers and the rapists and such that my mother and others warned me about. The powers that be made me leave my assigned room in The Towers building to walk to this "watchman duty" alone in the dark through the streets of Brooklyn with nothing to defend myself with, and with zero training in self-defense. On top of that, no one gave me any real instructions on what to do if I ever <u>did</u> find a bad guy during my watch, except run real fast and call somebody quickly.

So, there I was, stuck in an eerie bunch of factory buildings, walking around <u>in the dark</u> with only one measly flashlight on me that I was always worried would run out of batteries at any time. The factory had all sorts of places I could trip on or bump into or hurt myself somehow if I stepped in the wrong place. It was a factory after all and things shifted on a daily basis on each floor. I had to walk and climb for hours in the middle of the night, tired, lonely, and frightened that I could be in big trouble if I took a wrong turn or if I happened upon professional thieves who would most likely be grown men twice my size who would shoot me. On top of that, I had to look for these stupid keys which weren't always where they should be. To make matters worse, during all that time I was terrified because some jerks told me a horror story about the last dummy who got killed doing this insane exercise.

All I can say is, if you ever happen to visit the Bethel factory and chance upon the ghost of that poor dead Bethelite still roaming the vast cold crowded floors looking for his next key, tell him I said "Hi."

My GB can lick your GB

It was 1983 and Ronald Reagan was walking the halls of the White House as President of the United States. Meanwhile, Fred Franz was walking the halls of Bethel as the President of the Watch Tower Bible and Tract Society. Unlike the U.S. in the last one hundred years or so which had many presidents during those years, Fred W. Franz was only the fourth president of The Society ever, following Charles T. Russell, Joseph F. Rutherford, and Nathan H. Knorr. (Note: I will use real names for the references to the Governing Body members mentioned in these stories, with a few obvious exceptions.)

Fred Franz had just turned ninety years old and somebody asked him, "Brother Franz, how old does a man have to be before he loses interest in women?" Brother Franz answered in his very old man's voice, with a sly grin on his face, "Well, I don't know. You'll have to ask somebody older than me."

I didn't hear this particular exchange with Brother Franz personally, and although this story was only a few days old since it happened, it was told and retold repeatedly; it was already a legend around Bethel. Everybody laughed at this since it was well known Brother Franz loved to be surrounded by the ladies. I'm not implying he was a playboy, as I have no reason to believe he was anything but chaste with all the women that doted over him. He did love attention from the sisters though, that much was obvious. It was also well known he was one of the few single Governing Body members who never married, although he showed considerable interest in women none-the-less. This was always an issue of curiosity to me, a question that never had an answer. Couldn't he have found just one woman to marry in all those ninety years? With all the women who came through Bethel year after year, wasn't there even one who he could take a chance on marrying?

81

He would die after I left Bethel, just short of his one-hundredth birthday, still single. So I guess the answer was, "No." Since he was a chaste Christian from his youth on, and never married, it is highly likely that he died a virgin.

I only met Brother Franz twice, but it was always when dozens of people were surrounding him. As a result, I never spoke to him in any sort of conversational way. He would just sit and take in all the attention people gave him, with a sort of staring off into the distance kind of look that can usually be observed in people who were blind. Brother Franz was losing his eyesight by that time, and this was evident to me by his clothes, which looked a bit threadbare, although quite clean. He always seemed to dress in clothes that would have been odd looking even when they were new, I guess since his style of dress was probably set in his youth. They were cheap, even for a Jehovah's Witness, most of which wore inexpensive clothes. But also, they were a bit nerdy looking, even by the relatively unsophisticated JW standards of dress.

It's funny, but many considered him to be the most influential of all Governing Body members in the history of Jehovah's Witnesses, even over all other past Watch Tower Society presidents, with the possible exception of Charles T. Russell, the founder of the faith. Fred Franz joined Bethel during its earlier years in 1920, and was a useful editor and writer of JW literature almost from the beginning. His life spanned the second and third presidencies of The Society. He even did some "ghost writing" for these presidents, eventually becoming the fourth President himself.

I say it's funny because by the time I met him, he was to me just a very old, frail and tiny man in cheap scraggly clothes. Had I seen him on the street, I would not have thought one minute about this fairly diminutive, scrawny old guy with a chiseled set of skeletal German features. Yet, at the time when I met him, he may have had more influence on the Jehovah's Witness faith in the last seventy years than any other single human being. I would personally assert he was the most powerful Jehovah's Witness who ever lived, due to all the influence he had even before his presidency. Heck, it was a well known yet unpublished "fact" that he pretty much single handedly translated the Jehovah's Witness Bible called *The New World Translation of the Holy Scriptures*, even though he never really had the credentials or schooling to do this kind of translating work to begin with. Sure, he had help with a "committee," and he was sanctioned to do this translating by the president before him, I'll grant that. In the end though, when a person can complete a translation of their own Bible under their own authority and then get millions of people to not only use it exclusively, but to declare it to be better than any other Bible ever translated, well, I would call that power.

☆

Another Governing Body member I recall living at that time and who has since died, was Brother S-. The most notable thing about Brother S- was his eyebrows. It was hard to look at him or talk to him without staring at his eyebrows, because they looked like giant caterpillars crawling across his otherwise mostly bald-headed expanse of a forehead. When he talked, these eyebrows moved, which was actually kind of disconcerting because they caused you to fear that maybe they would crawl off his face and onto you. Why his wife or somebody else didn't gently suggest to him to trim those bad boys... I can't say. I can only think that maybe they did tell him, and Brother S- did trim them, only to have them grow back. Overnight.

Brother S- was also known for using salty language around the young guys and for being a closet racist. You see, most of the GB came from the generation when the black man knew "his place," and although The Society preached a good game about racial equality, it wasn't really reflected in the white faces of the men who ran everything. It wouldn't be until the JW faith was over 110 years old that there would eventually be even one black Governing Body member at all. Make no mistake, this black JW leader would not be the President though. Heck, even our worldly U.S. government has done better than God's House has in that regard, by electing a half black man to the helm of the United States of America. You would think that God, being color blind Himself, would have done a better job of choosing His leaders to reflect the true makeup of His people. After all, from a percentage perspective, white people are a minority on this planet, so why do they run everything in God's House?

Oh well, it is said that God moves in mysterious ways. (Although this is not exactly a scriptural quotation.) His preferring white people over the "darkies" to get His will done was evidently one of those mysteries.

The reason I bring up Brother S-'s racism is because it was widely known that he freely used the word "nigger" to talk about black people. Not "negro" and not "colored" mind you, rather, he used "nigger." Keep in mind that at that time it would be many years before even blacks would embrace this word among themselves. Even to this day, after all the history behind the use of this word, it would still be common sense that old white guys shouldn't use "the N word" at all.

Just saying.

Of course, Brother S- didn't use this term in public settings, like say from the podium at an assembly, or even at the Bethel breakfast table. Oh no. Like all discreet racists, he made sure this kind of talk was used in smaller private situations. I once attended a wedding he presided over, and the folks getting married were a very "southern," very "white," JW couple who were supposedly "very close" to Brother S-, at least according to the bragging bride. I guess they must have been close for Brother S- to perform their wedding in the first place, so I didn't doubt this claim of hers. I knew the bride fairly well, and while attending the wedding and in front of many people, I pointed out a neat looking lawn jockey figure she had at her house that had caught my eye. To this she commented, "Oh, yes. That's my little 'nigger man', isn't he cute?" I didn't know how to respond to that.

I suppose she thought that was an endearing term for the thing. After that, I concluded that was just the way people spoke in the privileged, white, JW circles that Brother S- ran in.

☆

Another GB member who stands out to me was Karl Klein, also since deceased. This was the Governing Body member most against Bethelites working out in a gym lifting weights, playing sports, going to parties, having fun of any kind or simply having any kind of life whatsoever.

To me, the main dig Brother Klein seemed to make was against the existence of our weight room at Bethel. He just couldn't see what use that room was for us Bethelites, and he said its only purpose was to serve our vanity. Fortunately for those of us who liked that place, the rest of the GB disagreed with him and let us keep it. That didn't mean he couldn't say these things at the breakfast table from time to time, thereby giving us angst each time he brought it up, causing us to worry that the weight room or even the rest of the gym might be closed down at his insistence.

☆

Back in those days, two other Governing Body members George Gangas and Dan Sydlik were still alive and walked the Bethel halls as well. These two Governing Body members could not have been more different from each other. Now, keep in mind when reading the following stories that Governing Body members were practically worshipped among Jehovah's Witnesses, as there was no one higher on the JW food chain than they were. Besides, it was thought that they had a direct line of communication with God Himself. How could you be bigger than that? It was like hobnobbing with Moses or Abraham.

Dan Sydlik at the time usually played the voice of God in most of the convention dramas. (As mentioned before, conventions were large annual gatherings of Jehovah's Witnesses.) The JWs who ran these conventions often re-enacted various Bible stories through mini plays (called dramas) and everybody in these dramas dressed up like ancient Israelites to make the stories more realistic. Those dramatic stories were retold through realistic sets, acting, music, and so on. It turns out that Brother Sydlik used to be the favorite voice of God in these dramas since he was a large man with a big booming voice, not unlike what it might sound like if you took the actor James Earl Jones and plugged him into an amplifier.

I can practically hear Sydlik now in the drama about Moses and the burning bush: "Moeeeses, Moeeeeses! Do not coooome neeeear heeeere. Remoooove the saaandals from your feeeet."

Dan Sydlik had a very self confident, outgoing personality. He walked powerfully and spoke with authority, even more so than most of the other GB. He also had a wife about half his age, which always tickled us young Bethelites. At least one GB was probably having hot sex in their room, we thought.

One day he gave a special invitation-only "New Boys" talk to us first year Bethelites. In this talk, he mentioned that we all needed to "roooound out our personaaaalities because Jehooooovah doesn't like squaaaare things." He said, "Look at naaaature, nothing is square in naaaature, this shows God loves smooooothness." Interesting I thought. I went up to him after that talk and making my way through the crowd surrounding him, I said:

Me: Loved the talk Brother Sydlik. But, regarding the square things in nature issue, I can think of something square in nature.

Sydlik: [eyeballs me for a second] Ohhhhhhh? Whaaaat?

Me: [confidently] Sodium Chloride. Table salt. It's a perfect cube. [I smile]

Sydlik: [grabs my tie and pulls me closer to his face] Whaaat's your naame boooy? If you're wronnng, there's a job chaaange in it for you! [playing at being mad]

Crowd: HaHaHaHa.

Me: [smiling, knowing he is playing] My name is Brock, sir. And it's Sodium Chloride. [now tickled pink with this]

Sydlik: [letting go of me seeing as I am getting the joke that he's pretending to be mad at me] Har, har, har! Gooood one, boy! [walks off]

☆

Now Brother George Gangas on the other hand was a little, hunched over Yoda-looking man who appeared to be about 200 years old. Like Fred Franz, he was another GB member who never married, and who also liked attention from the ladies. His voice was quieter than most of the GB and he seemed to be used much less than the rest of the GB was used. (In JW vernacular, "being used" meant specific assignments within the organization.) For example, the GB members would take turns each week leading us in the reading of what we called "the daily text," yet I don't recall Brother Gangas ever doing this. (A "daily text" was a once a day scriptural reading with an appropriate commentary on that scripture.) Maybe it was due to the fact that he sounded so funny when he spoke, or maybe it was because we heard that Gangas gave the rest of the GB a hard time and didn't always toe the line,

I don't know. Whatever the reason, it was rare to see him used in the same way as the other GB members.

In fact, sometimes you would not even see George Gangas listed as a Governing Body member at all on some JW lists. It's almost like he was the "token" GB guy, one chosen to show that you didn't have to be German, English, or American to be on that exclusive body. He proved that you could be a hard to understand little Greek guy, and still make it to the top of the JW hierarchy.

Brother Gangas was meek and retiring for the most part, except for when he spontaneously wanted to quiz you on random Bible trivia and then he would be very aggressive. Many a young Bethelite would be minding his own business and would come within range of Brother Gangas who would zero in on him and pounce. I was a recipient of this more than once myself. This is how it would go with the typical Bethelite caught in his sights:

Gangas: You, brother! [pointing, crooked finger, crooked smile, spoken in a slow staccato voice at first] CAN...YOU...TELL... ME... [pause, then faster] WHAT... are the seven creative days?!?!

Bethelite: What are whaaaa?

Gangas: [spoken in that old Greek man's voice again but a bit more clearly] WHAT... are the seven creative days?!

Bethelite: Oh, ummm, lessee...

Gangas: [staccato voice again, leading him to the answer] ...AND... GOD... SAID... LET... THERE... BE...

Bethelite: LIGHT!

Gangas: [beaming smile] Yes! Next!

Bethelite: Ummm...

And so it would go. After getting through all seven creative days, George would smile his Yoda smile and shuffle away.

He was a sweet and mostly harmless man, but he loved those questions. You probably shouldn't debate with him on the answers to those questions because that was one sure way to fire him up since he felt he knew these topics better than anybody did. In the years I was there, he would usually ask about the thirteen covenants, the twelve tribes of Israel, the twelve apostles, and so on, always seemingly mostly fixated on Bible trivia that was a list of some kind. Some of us got used to this questioning and even made up a Gangas cheat sheet. It was a small card with the answers to his most commonly asked questions and we would study it. When he would ask us the questions, we would pretend to struggle with the answers, but in the end just barely remember them, much to his delight. It didn't matter if he asked you the same questions before, he never seemed to remember to whom he asked what. It was always totally new to him each time he engaged somebody in this, and he always found joy in it.

★

I liked both Sydlik and Gangas, as they were real people and did and acted pretty much as they pleased, but in a good way. They seemed completely oblivious to the stodgy, careful, and calculated way many "Bethel Heavies" handled themselves. ("Heavies" meant important people like the GB or the many Bethel "committee" members.) They also seemed to have a genuine love of people that I didn't see in many of the other prominent Bethelites at that time.

I'd like to relate a story now about both of these GB members that was told to me second hand, that I think explains them very well. I didn't experience this myself, but it became part of the Bethel lore, and I did know people there who personally swore this happened.

One day the Bethel family had a particularly long day as they were up together late for some reason and were all heading back to their rooms. It just so happened that Brother Sydlik, Brother Gangas, and a few other Bethelites all got onto the same elevator to go back to their rooms. The doors shut and Brother Gangas turned and looked at one of the Bethelites, never missing an opportunity to pounce:

Gangas: You, brother! CAN... YOU... TELL...

Sydlik: [voice booming] CAN IT, GEOOOORGE! WEEE'RE ALL TIIIIRED!

Gangas: [looks down sadly, doesn't say another word]

The elevator got quiet and then the door opened, Sydlik strode out, and Gangas shuffled after him. A few others got out too.

When the doors closed again, those remaining in the elevator all looked at each other and then burst into laughter.

Seven brides for seven sorcerers

One day, the Governing Body came up with a really neat idea: Bethel Family Movie Night! Yes, the GB would hand pick a movie and show it to the entire Bethel family through our video broadcast feed so that we would watch it together. We could sit with our friends where we wanted to, dressed comfortably, and be munching on our favorite treats. This was a great idea since there were so many things Bethelites were told they could not do, it was refreshing just to have something chosen for us. With this, we didn't have to think about the many guidelines, rules and counsel involved in our choice of entertainment, we could just sit back and enjoy.

The first movie chosen for us was *Seven Brides for Seven Brothers*. Now, this would not have been a movie that I would have chosen to watch on my own. I was not into musicals; I don't think many twenty-year-old males are. If I had my choice, I would have been out watching the original movie *Tron* or maybe *Rocky III*, which were out at the movies at that time, but I had no money to see them. Since we were all going to gather together and watch this musical as one family, with our food and drinks and so on, I thought, "Sure. Let's do it." Well, many attended, including me. I have to say, the "movie night" idea was a huge success. Everybody who attended went back to their rooms in good spirits. Good times!

Encouraged by their recent success, the GB set up a second movie night for us soon after that. It was going to be a Disney cartoon called *Fantasia*. Now, this movie is a bit unusual in that it really is a clever way to expose children to classical music. If you haven't seen it, then let me describe the movie here. It is a cartoon made up of separate small stories (or sequences) set to classical music. Each short story cartoon has a theme that is matched to the music of a different classical composer. Most of these stories are simple flights of fantasy about frolicking animals and various plants coming to life and so on. Everyone thought that this would be perfect; we would watch a Disney movie at Bethel that the GB themselves had picked out.

I'd like for you to keep in mind that the Governing Body was thought to be the representatives of the 144,000 people chosen to go to heaven. This class of people was also referred to as "The Faithful and Discreet Slave," often shortened to "The Slave." With this kind of heavy backing, what could possibly go wrong with this choice for a movie at Bethel? Again, we thought we could just sit back and enjoy the show without all the usual angst surrounding choices in entertainment that Jehovah's Witnesses usually had. (Remember my problem with music in a previous story?)

Happily, we all gathered to watch the movie *Fantasia*. We were all enjoying ourselves as we previously did with the first movie until a sequence in the movie came up entitled *The Sorcerer's Apprentice.* When it came on, the Sorcerer was doing the magic stuff that Sorcerers do, with dramatic waving of the hands and with smoke and fire. This started some buzzing amongst the viewers in the Bethel rooms right away. Then, Mickey Mouse, who was the Sorcerer's apprentice, got a hold of the Sorcerer's hat and started to try to perform magical feats using it. Basically, Mickey was trying to get his tedious job of mopping and cleaning done by enchanting the mops and pails to do the work by themselves. Well, Mickey was not very good at magic, so all heck broke loose and everything went out of control, and, well, that's the fun of the story.

Unfortunately, this wasn't very fun for the Bethel family. This particular story sequence is near the beginning of the movie *Fantasia* and it was only one small part of the entire movie itself because each story lasted only a few minutes. We had already witnessed a few other stories, so anybody watching this should have known it would be over in a few minutes. Also, everybody knew that this story was based on fantasy, as most Disney movies were. You know, Walt Disney, the guy famous for witches and apples, spells and princesses, talking animals, and so on. This is not a new idea to anybody with half a brain who had ever seen anything by Walt Disney.

Still, given all that, it did not stop many in attendance from actually walking out of the movie! Yes, folks, you heard me right, the GB got a taste of their own medicine when they found out that their own subjects were more pious, more holy, and more spiritual than they were. These subjects simply wouldn't watch this GB sanctioned, personally hand-picked movie. This was all due to a cartoon mouse that pretended to do magic for a few minutes in an obvious flight of fantasy for which Walt Disney was beloved. This is because to the typical JW, magic was a big no-no. Remember me telling you all the restrictions JWs placed on each other? This was one of them. It was because the Bible condemns the practice of magic, that is, real magic. But that meant to the pious JW that even fanciful cartoon pretend magic was off limits.

At first, I was irked about this. I watched the movie anyway, regardless of the others who left in a snit. This was very confusing to me. "Darn it," I thought. "Bethel showed us all a movie and I was going to watch it." I had never seen it before, and I had looked forward to it, so no amount of guilt-ridden piety would keep me from seeing it. I must say, I enjoyed that movie quite a bit too.

Afterwards, in the ensuing days at Bethel, I witnessed and participated in many discussions on the subject of conscience matters due to the mass walk out this movie caused right in Bethel itself! I was amused at the extreme difference of opinion on this issue with people who otherwise almost always agreed on things. These were people who usually toed the robotic JW line and always said the same things in the same way as if reading them straight from the *Watchtower* magazine. Now, these otherwise agreeable automatons were in heated dispute about this silly little cartoon!

These discussions went something like this:

Brother 1: We should not watch anything to do with magic, the Bible says... blah blah blah.

Brother 2: It's a cartoon for heaven's sake. It's fantasy, pretend. All Disney is like that. It's not real magic that we were participating in... blah blah blah.

Brother 1: It doesn't matter if it is real or not. It has a demonic theme and overtone... blah blah blah.

Brother 2: Look, the GB saw fit to show it and they thought it was OK, so they obviously don't think it is demonic... blah blah blah.

Brother 1: It doesn't matter what other people think is OK. If it has images of spiritism or magic in it, then it is not fit for a Christian and is not OK with me. I won't watch it... blah blah blah.

Me: [having fun butting in] Really, Brother 1? It doesn't matter what other people think? We're not talking about just any "other people," we're talking about the Faithful and Discreet Slave here. These are the very people who we live our every moment listening to and obeying. So, let me get this straight: you'll let a family member die by not giving them a blood transfusion because of what The Slave says and you'll shun your own mother or father if The Society deems them as unrepentant sinners. But when these same men put a cartoon in front of you to watch, you are now in a quandary? Would you walk out of a *Watchtower* study based on these same principles you are now holding if you didn't agree with what the magazine was saying?

Well, we never really got anywhere with these discussions and this issue became a third rail of topics with emotions running high almost every time it came up. Most Bethelites, exhausted from the arguing, simply ended up agreeing to disagree on this issue and to put it to a "matter of conscience." Nobody wanted to touch this discussion anymore because of its volatility.

Of course, me being the smart acre I was, I took this as a cue that this should be the case for all matters of conscience. This included my wanting to watch R rated movies, my wanting to go to college, or to play sports at school or my choices in who and how I should date, what music I listened to, and many other personal things I thought were simply nobody else's business. These were all things every JW I knew tried to control my choices in by telling me what to do on a constant basis. But really, shouldn't they simply be a matter of each Christian's personal choice?

In the end, I was glad the issue with this Disney movie came up. You see, if anybody at Bethel ever again started to counsel me about something that was a personal matter of conscience, I would simply remind them: "Remember *Fantasia.*"

That would shut 'em up.

I saw you look at my daughter, now let's plan the wedding

When I was at God's House all those years ago, the "sisters" would visit in droves. I don't know if they do that now, but back then those ladies would sometimes come in actual bus loads to visit Bethel. Of course, they all said they were interested in seeing the headquarters where Jehovah's will was done, or they wanted to see where the *Watchtower* was written to get an appreciation for the Faithful and Discreet Slave. But, we all knew that was bull.

They mostly came to meet guys.

Now, as a young man full of testosterone, this was a good thing. I liked the attention when I got it, so even though there was a bazillion single brothers at Bethel, if you had any measure of looks at all, or had any game at all, you could have lots of sisters writing you, visiting you, and sending you stuff. Still, you had to be careful. If you were percieved as the playboy type, you would be labeled as such and the elders in the congregation would not "use" you for certain privileges, which would hurt your chances of ever being somebody in the congregation. Even if you didn't really date these sisters, or didn't really do much of anything at all with them, just by having more than one sister write to you or visit you, well, you could be labeled a playboy that way too, and possibly not be "used" because of that.

I got a taste of this very early on in my journey at God's House. When I first moved to Bethel I was assigned to a four-man room. My three older roommates approached me one day to have an ice cream party with them, just us four guys. I thought this was a nice idea until I realized this "party" was actually an "intervention" directed at me. You see, they had noticed that I was writing more than one girl at the same time and so they told me they were concerned about me because of it. The gist of this concern was that I wasn't showing proper respect for these girls because each

96

could think I was serious about them when I actually wasn't. They said that kind of behavior was not what a Christian man should display. I tried to explain that these girls were just friends. They replied that men and women couldn't be friends and that I was fooling myself about that. They opined that I was probably hurting these women emotionally. Please note: I was <u>not</u> promising them love, I was <u>not</u> dating them, and I was not even getting intimate with them in my letters in any way. I was just writing small talk to them. It didn't matter. My concerned roommates strongly suggested I curb this destructive behavior right away! (Needless to say, I got out of this four-man room arrangement as soon as I could.)

That said, it was a much more dire situation should you actually date a sister than simply write to her. That was a pretty serious thing to do because to a JW, especially a Bethelite, dating was S-E-R-I-O-U-S! You did not casually date in Bethel or even want to be known for <u>maybe</u> casually dating, at all. For example, if you dated a girl and it didn't work out, you had better not date another girl for a very long time. On top of that, you should act very mournful about the breakup, otherwise you could be labeled a playboy who casually toyed with women.

Furthermore, if you dated longer than a certain time (say six months) then you had better start thinking about getting engaged, otherwise you were obviously not a serious spiritual man, and would be seen as playing with her affections. This too could cause you to be labeled and not used in the congregation for special privileges.

Furthermore still, if you got engaged, you better get married fairly quickly after that, otherwise you were not taking your engagement seriously and would be labeled and not used for that reason either. Also, breaking an engagement was almost like divorce in the JW world. (By the way, divorce was strictly forbidden as a JW, except for adultery being committed by one of the parties.) In Bethel, if you broke an engagement, well, you most likely would be asked to leave, and would probably face serious repercussions once you returned home.

This actually happened to one of my pious roommates. He was one of those guys that fed me the ice cream and told me not to write to more than one girl at a time. Ironically, a few months after that intervention he arranged for me, he told me in confidence about a problem that developed with his own love life. It turns out that because he kept to his strict one-woman-at-a-time rule to the extreme, he found himself engaged to a woman he said "lied to him" about many things, including her desire to come to Bethel to be with him. After they were engaged, she told him she wasn't going to live in that "horrible place" (meaning Bethel). She allegedly said that there was nothing he could do about it now because they were engaged. She told him that she knew they would kick him out of Bethel once they were engaged, but then didn't marry. So, she allegedly said, he might as well leave Bethel on good terms to marry her, rather than not marry her and get kicked out anyway. Shotgun type weddings and other forced marriages were common among Jehovah's Witnesses for reasons just like this.

Tell me, do you see the problem here? When you were in The Truth, dating a girl even once set you up for a situation where you were rushing into marriage before you knew it. Even some poor souls who didn't actually "date" were forced to marry if they "toyed" with a girl's feelings, or a guy met a girl at a party and made out with her or groped her. If the girl's JW father had enough status in the congregation, and the JW boy had status in the congregation to lose, well, this could actually be more intimidating than holding a shotgun to the young guy's head.

Most of us knew the deal. We were very careful about who we talked to, because of where it could lead to and very quickly. So, we protected ourselves by doing things in groups. If a guy liked a girl, he asked her and her friends to do stuff with him and his friends. Everybody was in on it. Officially, nobody was "dating" because nobody was alone with anybody else. It came down to the fact that we basically dated in packs to keep the official "dating" issue at arm's length, thus giving us plausible deniability if pressed on the subject.

Well, one day, one of my friends at Bethel introduced me to a few girls he knew who were visiting from New Jersey. I thought one of these girls was especially cute, and wanted to spend more time with her than I had during her short Bethel visit. The problem was I had just gone out the week before with other girls (also in a group) and I didn't want to do that again too soon. So, I asked my friend to set up another group get together in order for me to see this new girl again. I cautioned him not to make it too soon however. Meanwhile, I would be writing this new girl a few letters to tide me over and to get to know her better, but making sure not to brazenly write other girls during this same time period.

My friend made the arrangements, and a month or so later, during our once-a-month Saturday off, we went to New Jersey to visit this girl. Of course, we also met with her friends in our now safe "not really dating" group. There were the two of us guys, and it turns out three girls, all meeting at the girl's house who I wanted to get to know better. Let's call this girl Cutie Smith.

Cutie and her friends greeted us upon arrival. She brought us into her kitchen and introduced us to her mom, her dad, and her brothers. They were all really nice, and the girl was even cuter than I remember her being the first time I met her. The casual clothes she wore that day showed off her figure much more than what I saw at Bethel, and she actually looked better without all the make-up she had on the first day I met her. She just had a simple, natural, girl-next-door beauty that I was pleasantly surprised to see. On top of it all, she turned out to be a real sweetheart of a person as well. The letters I received from her actually reflected the very decent girl I was seeing in front of my eyes now. "Wow, this was one nice girl," I thought. "This was going to be a great day!"

After a time, all the five young folks went outside to play, that is, my friend, Cutie and her friends, and me. We were having a great time. It snowed earlier and we played in it. We threw snowballs and ran and laughed and talked and joked around. This was great clean fun. Cutie paid extra attention to me and I was eating it up. She was a great flirt, but not over the top with it. She was just perfect about how you would want a girl to show interest in you without being intimidating or pressuring. This was only the second time I had a chance to see Cutie, but I was starting to think that maybe there could be something there. Just by the way she looked at me, my hormones were on full alert.

I was even thinking about how I might stop writing to any other girls, because I thought there might be a strong possibility that I could focus on Cutie. Of course, I would have to take this slow and be careful because of the stupid JW and Bethel rules about such things, but this could be one girl worth taking a chance on. I could just tell she wasn't a trouble making kind of girl, and that was important to me at the time. I wasn't certain as to whether or not this would work out because I had just met her. "Maybe it was just physical?" I thought. "Who knows?" I was looking forward to figuring it all out, as I could only see pleasant times ahead for the both of us.

Well, this euphoria all came crashing down on my head when I went inside to get a drink of water. Her mother was alone in the kitchen making us lunch and I asked her for water. The ensuing conversation went something like this:

Mom: [sweetly] Sure hon, I can get you water. Let me get you some hot chocolate too. Would you like some?

Me: Sure! Thanks!

Mom: Great. [hands me a glass of water.] So, how are you and Cutie getting along?

Me: Fine. She's a real nice girl, Sister Smith. [drinks the water]

Mom: [preparing the hot chocolate] So, you like her then?

Me: Sure, um, I like her.

Mom: A lot?

Me: [getting a bit uncomfortable] Um, well, sure. I mean we just met and all, but I suppose so. You know, it takes time to get to know someone.

Mom: So, you don't like her a lot then?

Me: No. Um, yes. I mean, well, we just met, right?

Mom: You don't sound sure.

Me: Well, I'm sure I'll be having fun getting to know her more.

Mom: Oh, so that's it? You're just having "fun" with her?

Me: No. I didn't mean it that way, I...

Mom: Really, you Bethelites, trifling with young girls nowadays. These poor girls really like a brother and the brothers just play with their feelings.

Me: What? No. I'm not trying to play with her feelings, Sister Smith. We've just got to know each other for a few hours so far, that's all.

Mom: Oh, really? Then why are you dating her?

Me: Dating? When? We just met!

Mom: Well, what do you think this day is all about? You've been writing her, and now you're on a date right?

Me: Wow. Well, I thought we were all just getting to know each other in a group, you know, not dating, but just a group activity kind of thing...

Mom: Here's your hot chocolate. [hands it to me] Now, what you need to do is to be honest with yourself and to decide if you are going to date my daughter or not. Really, it's not that difficult. [smiles sweetly, though a bit forced]

Me: [timidly] Yes ma'am.

I left with my hot chocolate, stunned. The old bag had seen right through the "not really dating in a group" thing. She knew I liked her daughter, but wouldn't even give us the chance to pretend to "not date" for a while to see how things went. The mother made it clear to me that I had to make my decision about her daughter that very day: either declare that I was dating her, or let her be.

I remember stumbling outside, a bit confused. I just sat down on a fence near the house lost in thought, trying to figure out my next move. I was thinking that a mother-in-law that manipulative would be hell to deal with. I had actually been in a situation like this before my time in Bethel, where I dated an otherwise sweet girl, but her mother was a battle-ax and made my life miserable by trying to force our relationship to a place I was not ready for. That was not a nice situation to find myself in.

I looked over at Cutie Smith, laughing and playing in the distance. She spied me and then ran up and sat very close to me, brushing her shoulder against me teasingly. She then turned towards me, smiled sweetly, giggled and took my hot chocolate and sipped some of it. She looked at me admiringly.

I remember looking into her lovely eyes and thinking that it was a shame that this day would be the last time I'd ever see her.

Angels and Women, kind of like a Playboy

Ever since I could remember, I loved to read. Yes, I was one of those aggravating kids who all the other kids thought was a nerd because I loved books. I loved learning new things and reading about new worlds. So sue me.

Back when I was a kid, we didn't have the internet, so if you liked to read, then you liked libraries. Once I found myself in New York as a young man in Bethel, it was natural for me to eventually make my way to the New York Public Library. It was awesome. But, it was also a bit out of the way for me to get to, and I didn't have all that much spare time to make the trip very often. For me, the next best thing was going to the Bethel library.

Now, the Bethel library was nowhere near like any normal library in that you wouldn't necessarily find books by Agatha Christie or Ray Bradbury there. But, you could find things there that you couldn't find any other place. I remember one of the first things I found there was an old *Daily Text* book called *Daily Manna*. (The *Daily Text* is a JW book for daily scripture reading and commentary.) If I recall correctly, this book was from the early 1920s and it was similar to the current JW *Daily Text* books only written in a more old time looking font. But, the thing that struck me the most about that book was that it had a calendar in it and on that calendar were curious notations from an early-day Bethelite who owned that book. You see, on that calendar of the *Daily Manna* book were reminders of other people's birthdays! Excited, I quickly flipped over to December 25th and lo and behold, there was a notation about Christmas! With this, I was able to conclude that early Jehovah's Witnesses did in fact celebrate birthdays, and most holidays, just like everybody else.

Surprisingly, this discovery paled to insignificance when I found a book called *Angels and Women*. This was one of the most fascinating books I had ever seen in my young life. Since this time predated the internet, we were much more innocent about many things back then. I had never heard of this book before, nor had I conceived that a book like this might exist.

In order for you to understand why this book was so fascinating to me, I have since found the foreword to it, which I will share with you here. Since the foreword is very long, I will only share with you the first part of it in order for you to get an idea of what I read all those years ago in that quiet Bethel library, so you can see what hooked me right away.

Please note however, this book has an interesting history in that *Angels and Women* really is a rewrite of an earlier book called *Seola*. A random person not related to the Jehovah's Witness faith wrote this earlier book, *Seola*. However, the "reviser" of that book, the author of *Angels and Women*, actually is very much related to the Jehovah's Witness faith. You see, the foreword of *Angels and Women* says that its reviser is a personal friend (or confidant) of Pastor Charles T. Russell, which is the name of the founder of the JW faith. The book *Seola* was therefore revised under the suggestion of Pastor Russell himself.

The actual author of *Angels and Women* is not revealed, as is the author of most JW books. It is often left up to speculation as to who actually authors what books that come from the Watch Tower Bible and Tract Society. The general opinion has always been that the author of *Angels and Women* was a man by the name of J.F. Rutherford, the actual name of C.T. Russell's successor to the presidency of the Watch Tower Bible and Tract Society. (So, this book was revised by the second JW president and egged on to be done by the first JW president.) The opinion of Rutherford being the reviser of *Seola* is based on the fact that the theology, phrasing, and wording in the foreword could be found in Rutherford's other known writings.

Whatever the truth of this may be, it is a fact that whoever wrote *Angels and Women* (thus revising *Seola*) was a person definitely related to the Watch Tower Bible and Tract Society in a key way. Since Rutherford was the next guy on the JW totem pole who kept the JW faith burning after Russell died, this is a big deal. If Rutherford did in fact rewrite *Seola* to make a new book called *Angels and Women*, well, this had huge ramifications in the JW world. Once you find out the basis of how this book came to be in the first place, this actually becomes quite shocking.

So, here is the first part of the foreword from this fascinating book:

Angels and Women - The Foreword

TRITE but true is the saying, "Truth is stranger than fiction." Fiction sometimes illumines the truth.

A number of years ago Mrs. J. G. Smith published a Novel entitled *Seola*. She claims to have been impelled to write it after listening to beautiful music. She made no pretense of knowledge of the Bible. Yet so many of her sayings are so thoroughly in accord with the correct understanding of certain scriptures that the novel is exceedingly interesting and sometimes thrilling.

The greatest Bible scholar of modern times read this book shortly before his death. To a close personal friend he said: "This book, if revised according to the facts we know about spiritism, would be instructive and helpful." Long prior thereto this noted Bible scholar had written and published the first clear presentation of the Bible teaching on spiritism. He advised his personal friend to revise the novel *Seola* and to publish it if opportunity afforded at some future time.

This book deals with the events transpiring between the date of the creation of man and the great deluge. The principal characters figuring in the novel are Satan, fallen angels and women. Angels are heavenly messengers. There was a time when all angels were good. The time came when many of them allied themselves with Satan and became evil, hence called "fallen angels"... Evil spirit beings started good human beings on the downward road. Evil angels and bad women have made countless millions mourn.

The Bible story of fallen angels or evil spirits, is briefly told as follows: Lucifer, once a good spirit being...

I read those words and I was almost in a state of a trance. I just <u>had</u> to read this book!

You see, before going to Bethel, I was an avid reader of Greek mythology. I started reading mythology as a school assignment, but I ended up reading every single Greek and Roman mythology book or collection I could get my hands on. I loved this stuff. One of the main reasons I loved it was that some Bible commentators had postulated that all Greek mythology was rooted in actual fact, and that these were actually altered accounts of people who had witnessed the time before the flood. The "gods" of these mythology stories were actually demons (for example, Zeus was Satan) and the demi-gods, those born from the Gods and humans (like Hercules) where actually the Nephilim that the Book of Genesis talked about. I didn't know if this was true or not, and I still don't know, but I wanted it to be true. I absolutely ate this stuff up. Keep in mind that this theme was used in movies of that time too like *Clash of the Titans* and a couple of *Hercules* movies, so to me, this was a very current topic.

When I found *Angels and Women* at Bethel, why here was a book that claimed to be about pre-flood days, about (fallen) angels and the women about whom the Bible says, "They took all of whom they chose." (Genesis 6:2) Best of all, it was a JW book probably written by one of the Presidents of the JW organization! Wow! What could be better?

I used to ask myself all the time, what <u>would</u> it have been like to have lived back then before the flood? How did these angels (demons) act back then? What did they look like? How did they get the women? Did they seduce them or did they just grab them and carry them off by force? Did anybody fight back? If so, who? How? Why didn't these demons just kill Noah and his sons who were preaching negatively about them? Didn't these angels know these people? Weren't they powerful enough to kill them? Or, did God protect them somehow? And so on.

I used to ask myself those things all the time. This book, which claimed to be channeled by somebody who didn't even know the Bible, <u>had those answers</u>! Here, I could read about how Noah survived supernatural demonic attack. Here I could read about how the gorgeous, hulking, buffed-out angels acted and seduced or otherwise "took" gorgeous women to do what they wanted with them. Really cool!

So, I kept reading that book. I could not finish the first night I found the book, so the next time I got the chance I went back to read more. (We could not check books out of this particular library.) When I finished reading this book, I was thrilled and even shaking a little bit. It was <u>so</u> cool to read these things and, best of all, it was a "Society" book! Yes sir, it was right in the Bethel library and so I could quote from it from now on too, right?

Wrong.

I found out how wrong I was when I brought this up to one of my elders in a car ride to a meeting one day. When I excitedly brought up this book to him, there was silence by this elder at first. He then told me in a lowered voice that, "We should not be reading that book." What? Why? "Well," he said, "because that book has spiritism connections as its original manuscript was written with what is called 'automatic writing'." He went on to explain that the original book *Seola*, if authentic at all and not made up, can only be understood to have come from a demon itself and we should not be reading words from demons. If not authentic, then it was a sham, as it claimed to have supernatural authorship. So, you see, either way, we should not read it. Furthermore, we should not be talking about this book either due to the fact that true Christians should not have any connection to spiritism.

Bummer. I so wanted to talk about this book with somebody. I had so many questions, but according to this elder, nobody should talk to me about it. My mind reeled. "Wait a minute..." I thought. "Why in the heck would Pastor Russell and Brother Rutherford, our religion's founding fathers, get mixed up in a book that had a connection to spiritism?" This would be like finding out that George Washington and John Adams were mixed up in writing a book about communism. Hey, didn't that mean I read a book that might have been written by a demon? And enjoyed it?! Yikes! Why would The Society subject me to this sin by keeping the book in the library in the first place?

Well, this particular elder had no patience for me on much of anything in general, so I didn't push back much once he told me to drop it. I just politely asked him why the book *Angels and Women* was in the Bethel library in the first place. Although his answer was forgettable, I do recall saying to him in response: "Well, to me, then, this is like putting a *Playboy* magazine in the Bethel library and then telling us not to look at it."

He had no answer for that.

The Hanger Men also die

My journey was unexpectedly put in jeopardy at God's House when I got hurt. You see, it wasn't enough that most of us worked physically forty-four to sixty-five hours a week, and it wasn't enough that we walked literally miles a day through the streets of New York and the tunnels of Bethel. It also wasn't enough that many of us had a workout schedule in the gym on top of that. No, that simply wasn't enough activity for us. We also felt compelled to play sports to display our machismo to each other, even though the Bethel authorities frowned about it in general. Still, it wasn't strictly forbidden, so we did it.

My sport of choice was football, and on this particular day I did a number to my knee stepping in a pothole during a running play. The other players looked sheepish as various Bethel people tended to me, then helped me hobble to the infirmary. The doctors X-rayed and the nurses fussed. Soon, I was told I would need to be off my feet for about seven to ten days. They told me that in order for my knee to heal properly, I needed to rest it completely with no walking or even standing. Certainly, there would be no sports of any kind for me. "That wasn't so bad," I told myself. "It's only a few days." No big deal, right?

Well, it kind of was.

You see, for the time period I was healing, I would not be able to do my regular Bethel job due to the fact it required that I stood most of the time. Many senior Bethelites in the factory and elsewhere found the fact I hurt myself playing football extremely irritating. I didn't get it. Don't all people get hurt from time to time? Isn't that part of life? Certainly The Society's love for me would compel them to take care of me during my own time of need, right? Well, I got a lesson in how The Society felt about getting hurt like I did, during my visit to the infamous "Hanger Room."

The Hanger Room was located in the bowels of Bethel. When you go down into the Bethel tunnels that run beneath the streets of Brooklyn, you understand that you are underground, but you simply don't know the half of it. I found out to my dismay that there were other deeper levels previously unknown to me. The Hanger Room was evidently in the third level of Hell, compared to say the main laundry area which itself was a dim hole, but only located just beneath the ground. The Hanger Room was darker, danker, dingier, and dreadful and was located in the basement of one of the Society's bleakest buildings. This room wasn't actually physically lower than the other places in the Bethel tunnels, it just seemed like it was.

The room was also occupied and run by one of the most terrifying creatures in all Betheldom: **Brother Hanger Man**! [insert scary music here, followed by the sound of thunder]

I was sent to the Hanger Room because there I could be of some use while I convalesced. The Hanger Room was a place where they sent all the twisted up, bent, and broken hangers. Bethel used thousands upon thousands of hangers, every day. When any of them were deemed less than perfect, they were dropped into a chute and they slid down into a big bin, which eventually made its way into the Hanger Room. There, a brother so old that Methuselah would have called him grandpa, would snatch a hanger up, peer at it closely through a cloudy eye, and then begin CPR on the injured hanger. If it needed bending, he would bend it back with an appropriate tool and the correct bending technique. If it had problems with the paper bottom of the hanger, he would either repair that paper or replace it. Then, he would proudly put the restored hanger in a cart made for repaired hangers and move on to the next broken candidate. Bethel didn't waste anything, and the way they treated the Bethel hangers was an amazing example of this. Also, it gave Brother Hanger Man a job in his advanced age.

The Hanger Room was also where they sent bad little boys like me who were also twisted up, bent and broken, and who had to sit for a time convalescing. So, I got myself down there on my crutches and introduced myself to Brother Hanger Man. He just grunted at me and said, "C'mere." I got closer to him and noticed he smelled like week-old bacon left in the sun. He then proceeded to show me very quickly what he did with those hangers, and then abruptly said, "Now you do it."

I started to repair hangers with the Hanger Man. Time stood on end. I worked on these hangers and fixed what I thought was at least a thousand of them, then looked at the clock. Only twenty minutes had passed! Holy cow! The Hanger Room must be in a time warp or something. I began to fix my next hanger and tried to engage Brother Hanger Man in some conversation to pass the time. He just grunted at me. He seemed ticked off. At first, I just thought that maybe that was what old guys acted like when their age spots got so big they looked like human leopards. We toiled on until our first break. "Break time," he declared and scurried off. "Thank God," I thought. I was going out of my mind already and it was only the first break on the first day?!

After the break, we resumed our tedious work in silence. Now, as if it were possible, time actually seemed to go slower! "OK. Brother Hanger Man is messing with me," I thought. Since we were in the bowels below Hell itself and there was only one ancient clock to say what time it was, maybe he had adjusted that clock to run at one tenth speed? Or maybe time was different down here near the Earth's core? Perhaps the day was actually over and he was making me work in an endless loop, like some twisted *Twilight Zone* episode?

I was going batty. In order to keep my mind active, I tried to engage him in conversation. He grunted one word answers at me. "OK. So what's the deal? This <u>has</u> to be personal," I thought. I

112

decided to get more direct with him about this and it went something like this:

Me: Brother Hanger Man?

Him: Grunt

Me: Uh. Are you upset with me for some reason, sir?

Hanger Man: Grunt, mumble... appreciation... sassin frassin... disgraceful... mumble, grumble...

Me: Excuse me? What was that? Uh, you seem to be upset. Did I do something?

Hanger Man: [in his ancient voice that sounded like gargling phlegm] I SAID, you young brothers have no appreciation for things, mumble, grumble... always putting yourselves at risk. Hummina, hummina... Disgraceful if you ask me.

Me: Uhhh, at risk? What do you mean?

Hanger Man: Yes. You young people always go get hurt playing sports and fooling around and then cannot do your work! Grumble, mumble. You didn't come to Bethel so you could sit around like an old man like me. Snurf, snarf. You should be on your assignment, working like a young brother should be working. Hummina, hummina...

Me: Uhh. Well brother, it was an accident. I didn't hurt myself on purpose. I mean, I didn't do it to get out of my work.

Hanger Man: Hmmmffff. Mumble grumble, sassin frassin... young ne'er do goods... mumble, grumble... no respect... why, back in my day... frickin, frackin...

And so it was, Hanger Man was irked because one of the young Watch Tower grunts wasn't able to complete a normal grunt day.

He was annoyed that this young man had set back the entire organization and showed an obvious lack of appreciation and respect too. On top of it all, this young punk hurt himself needlessly, no check that, <u>probably on purpose</u>, just playing a silly game! How inconsiderate of this ne'er do well! This young 'un is costing The Society money in X-rays and bandages and food and everything! This will not be tolerated!

So, Hanger Man rightfully gave me a piece of his shaky mumbling mind. After that, it got quiet in that dank room with just me and the obviously peeved Hanger Man. I decided to just do my work, not argue with him and forget about it, as I watched that clock slowly tick by... slower and slower with each passing minute.

The day went on forever, and ever, and ever, and ever... and ever... and ever... and ever... and ever... and ever... and ever... and ever... and ever...

The next day I called up my floor overseer and <u>begged</u> him to let me back in the factory. I said I would glue books, sort papers, polish or clean stuff or do <u>whatever</u> I could during this down time of mine, but "Please, please," I pleaded, "Don't send me back to the hanger room." He said, "Sure. I'll figure something out." I never felt so happy to be able to do tedious factory nonsense work. Now I was at least able to do tedious factory nonsense work around guys my own age and in a building with natural light coming into it. Nobody there smelled like spoiled bacon either.

I also ended up getting back to my regular work much earlier than the seven to ten days the silly doctors said I would need. What did <u>they</u> know? Heck, the Bethel overseers put up with me and even let me limp around doing my regular job in pain. Luckily, I was able to do my job better and better each day, limping less and less. You see, the pain eventually worked itself out, so it was no big deal. I mean, it was a small price to pay even though decades later I <u>still</u> have problems with that knee, and it required me to have an operation on it after leaving Bethel at considerable expense to myself.

But who cares about all that? You see, the important thing was not to lose those crucial seven to ten days of making books and magazines for The Society by sitting around fixing hangers. So, I gladly suffered with the pain and permanent injury, and in return I would never have to see the Hanger Man again.

I look back on this now and can't help but wonder if that was simply all just part of the plan.

God loves a good double chocolate chip

As a young man in God's House, I used to skip out on the Bethel meals from time to time when I got tired of the same old same old they slung our way. For example, sometimes the Bethel Farms would get an extra good crop of apples by which they made good use of them in our meals. (Yes, The Society owned actual farms where they grew all their own food.) I used to like apples back then, until I had to eat them for every meal for a couple of months. By the time the Bethel kitchen was done with them, I hated apples.

Here's an example of a daily menu during apple season:

Breakfast: Eggs and an apple crusted ham, with baked apples, apple pastries, hot apple cider, and fresh apples for a snack break.

Dinner: Baked chicken and apple flambé, apple salad with applesauce, and apple juice, along with an apple crisp for dessert.

Supper: Left over apple flambé and baked apples, an apple slaw salad along with more apple cider and apple cobbler for dessert. They threw in dried apple strips for a take-home snack.

I finally knew how the Israelites felt eating manna every day.

Now, given the above, when the meal was particularly good, it went the other way. All Bethelites would come out of the woodwork to eat at the tables, sometimes fighting over the food. It seemed utterly ridiculous to me some Bethelites, usually older sisters, would use the Bible principle of "gleaning" to greedily take any and all of your food away from you. They did this if you didn't eat up fast enough and it was food they wanted. You see, gleaning was the practice ancient Jews used as a way to have mercy on the poor. Those who owned fields or orchards would be instructed by Mosaic Law to leave some of the crops and otherwise dropped or bruised fruits and lesser wanted grains in their fields or orchards, so the less fortunate who were hungry could come and collect (glean) what was left. This made sense in those days and was a fine provision that I am not making light of.

My complaint was with the big, plump 250+ pound Bethel sisters (who ate three square meals a day including dessert, as well as daytime and midnight snacks, who had obviously not missed a meal in years) would use "gleaning" to get even more food. You see, they would run over to your table right after the dismissal prayer, and snatch your chicken or pizza off your table's plate if you didn't finish it by prayer's end. They did this in the name of "gleaning," which they thought gave this selfish move a measure of nobility. If you dared say something to them, well, then you were the jerk, not them. I found the best defense for this was to go on the offense and to carry my own plastic container with me for the "better meals." So, once the GB gave the dismissal prayer and said "Amen," I could then immediately put any of my food into that container. I could also snatch up the food of any newbie who didn't know any better. "Hah! Take that, you greedy gobblers! Two can play at that game!"

Anyway, I skipped the more boring meals every once in a while and bought burgers or something else at a local place with the meager stipend I was given. I always felt guilty doing this because we were told that this showed something about "Not appreciating The Society's provisions, blah blah blah," but I did it anyway because I just couldn't take it sometimes. I mean, do you really want to even try to choke down under-seasoned, gristle-laden boiled beef?

Now, sometimes I might just eat the food I had in my room. I could buy some of it fairly cheaply at the Bethel Commissary. Yes, the place where we could buy food to take back to our rooms was named after what all institutions called it: a commissary. This was interestingly the same name a prison or military base would use for the same kind of place. So, I guess it was aptly named.

Anyway, I might have had a few things to eat stashed away, like the newly popular Hot Pockets or Jell-o Pudding Pops (early 1980s inventions) but most of the food in my room was junk food. That meant if I wanted to eat something a bit more substantial, I had to walk the streets of Brooklyn to get it.

One day, after a clandestine pizza lunch at Fascati's Pizza Parlor, I walked over to the local ice cream shop to get a cone. I got in line and waited my turn. The ice cream shop was fairly crowded and noisy at this time. I was musing over what flavor of ice cream cone I would get, when suddenly I was startled to hear God's voice booming out above the din:

God: YESSSS... I'LL HAAAVE A DOOOUBLE CHOOOOCOLATE CHIIIIP ON A SUUUUGAR CONE PLEEEEEASE!

Me: [jumping] What the...?

Well, it turned out it wasn't God after all. It was only Brother Sydlik. Since he played God in the dramas, his voice always sounded like God to me. To a new Bethelite, anyone on the Governing Body was kind of like God anyway. I realized that he was ordering ice cream here instead of eating the Bethel provided dessert and was therefore evidently "neglecting The Society's provisions" too. Cool! Now I didn't have to feel so bad about my doing the same. He even ordered the same flavor as I usually did.

When he passed me, I weakly called out to him, "Hey... Brother Sydlik..." Either he didn't see me, or he saw me and didn't acknowledge it. He just passed me by, licking his cone.

But that was OK. It was still nice to see that like me, God loves a good double chocolate chip.

Question The Society and your tongue will rot in your mouth

As far back as I can remember as a child, Armageddon was the most frightening thing in the world to me. Some children feared the boogeyman or ghosts, others the Chupacabra. Many feared monsters in their closets or under their beds. Some were scared of large animals, terrified of clowns or afraid of the dark.

Me? I worried about Armageddon.

Jehovah's Witnesses spoke of it often. Sometimes they depicted it in their literature, usually with buildings and cars falling into the earth, flames shooting out everywhere, people fighting with each other, and church steeples toppling from lightning strikes straight from heaven, with death everywhere. Sometimes, JW literature quoted Zechariah 14:12 to explain what might happen to the wicked during Armageddon, "Now this will be the plague with which Jehovah will strike all the peoples... their flesh will rot while they stand on their feet, and their eyes will rot in their sockets, and their tongue will rot in their mouth."

This was not only from the God of the Old Testament, as some people might argue. We also learned this from the God of the New Testament, as taken from the book of Acts chapter 12 verse 23: "Immediately, because Herod did not give praise to God, an angel of the Lord struck him down, and he was eaten by worms and died." So, given these scriptures, we could be sure the Christian God would also do the flesh rotting, carnivorous worm attack again at Armageddon. If you have ever seen the ending of the *Raiders of the Lost Ark* (which came out just before I left to Bethel) then you would have seen a glimpse of the JW future of the face melting, head exploding vengeance God would be wreaking on everyone very, very soon.

You tell me, can you think of anything more terrifying to a child than rotting where you stood? Or maybe being eaten alive by worms? Even if you didn't have this happen to you personally, did you really want to see this happen to other people? There was nobody I knew that I would wish that upon, but many Jehovah's Witnesses did. Some spoke quite often of people "getting theirs" during Armageddon.

For example, I recall one elder saying this in my youth when we had to move one of our meetings to a hotel because our Kingdom Hall was full. We wanted to celebrate the annual Memorial of Christ's Death (think Communion), but we didn't have the room for all the extra people who usually attended this service. (By the way, this is the only holiday JWs celebrate.) So, we booked a large hotel conference room for this event. That evening we found out that the hotel spelled our God's name Jehovah incorrectly on the nice sign they set up to welcome us. Instead of being appreciative that the hotel was trying to be welcoming, this elder turned to me and said with an evil grin, "Well, they're going to know who Jehovah is when they get theirs. Maybe then, they will spell His name correctly, just before they die."

To me, many Jehovah's Witnesses seemed to be good with the idea of everybody else dying around them during this terrifying time. I always dreaded it, even if I were safe myself. It just seemed all too horrible and traumatic. I didn't look forward to it at all, and part of me felt I wasn't really any better than everybody else was anyway.

Now, one of the main reasons we were sure that Armageddon was imminent back then was because of The Society's understanding of End Times Prophecy. You see, Jehovah's Witnesses had it all figured out. We called the world as we lived in it right now "this system of things." We pretty much knew when the end of this system of things was coming, as we could easily calculate it by doing simple math. By doing this math, we knew that God would be raining down His wrath on people any minute now. This was the time to get your act together like I did: stop messing around with girls, quit college and other selfish pursuits in a dying ungodly world, and start making Bible literature! STAT!

I will not bore you with the details of how Witnesses were sure about some of the dates they often used to calculate the end, but suffice it to say that 1914 was a key date in JW prophecy. They believe that in 1914, Jesus came back to Earth. Actually, according to initial JW prophecy, this was the first date given for Armageddon to come. Once "the end" didn't come, they then said it was an "invisible coming" instead. Unfortunately, nobody else could tell that Jesus "returned" except Jehovah's Witnesses. The 1914 date also started the clock on what we called "this generation." When you take this date, then all you needed to do was add the clue that Jesus gave us in Matthew 24:34 which states, "This generation will not pass until all these things occur." So, you see, if 1914 was the beginning of "this generation" because Jesus had come, then the earthquakes and wars since that date simply marked notches in the time line until the end of our known world, the end of this system of things.

The question then became very simple: How long is "this generation" that Jesus was talking about? Well, that's easy too! Psalms 90:10 says, "As for the days of our life, they contain seventy years, or if due to strength, eighty years." So, you see, that's the longest a "generation" could be, and we would know when our world would end by doing this math: 1914 + 70 or at the most 1914 + 80. This meant we could expect Armageddon to come, on the outside, around 1984 to 1994. On the outside, mind you! It could even be before that!

But wait, there's more! The Society also said that in order to be really part of "this generation" you had to be old enough in 1914 to understand what was happening in the world, not just be a baby. Therefore, if you shaved off 10 to 12 years from that (the age where you could "understand" what was happening), then that meant Armageddon would be all that much closer. Now, you do the math. Take 1994 (the absolute outside date that we can expect Armageddon) and subtract 12 and you get 1982, or subtract 10 and you get 1984. Guess what? I was living in those years at that time! This was a date that The Society said was on the outside for the time for Armageddon!

People, let me tell you, we knew this thing was going to blow any minute!

Well, during our Bethel breakfast one day, the presiding GB was reading our daily text, which mentioned "this generation" in it. In the commentary of this Bible reading that particular day, there was a quick review of the information I just gave you. The text was admonishing us to stay alert because "the end of this system of things was near," as our generation was "soon coming to a close." After all, we could easily see that by doing the math I just shared with you.

For some reason, that morning, the entire calculation around 1914, the entire reasoning behind what a "generation" meant, all of it, just became a big question mark in my brain. I couldn't help but think, "Boy, what if they're wrong?" The Society had admitted previously that it was "sort of" mistaken about many other dates it had given to Jehovah's Witnesses in past decades in the history of our religion, but they glossed over those mistakes by simply saying that, "The path of the righteous was like a light getting brighter and brighter until the day came fully." (Proverbs 4:18) You see, these were not mistakes, they were "adjustments." They instructed us that we could make "adjustments" in our beliefs and that was OK.

However, that day at breakfast, it came to me that I was hinging everything upon these particular dates. I wasn't so happy about the possibility of spending my entire youth making books in a cold factory, only to have them tell us later when I was an old man, "Oops, remember that 1914 + 70 or 80 years thing? Well, we have some new 'light' for you on that and need to make a few 'adjustments'..."

Because of this feeling, I brought it up at breakfast that morning to my table head GS-. (Remember, this was the man who was on the Writing Committee and who had a personal hand in writing the *Watchtower* and other JW literature.) I mainly questioned the definition of "this generation" by asking if perhaps we could think of a generation in a much broader sense. I also questioned the 1914 date as being the start of "this generation." I used a number of reasoning points with him that morning based on some of the things I have just explained.

Well, the other people at the table who heard my questions and comments were aghast. I recall GS-'s wife looking at me in horror when I brought it up. You see, this was bordering on apostasy to question what The Society teaches. Apostates are the worse people of all in the JW world, worse than even DF'd people. Way beyond DF'd actually. You could get reinstated if you were disfellowshipped and not be disfellowshipped any longer. Apostates were simply doomed, period. Any JW who outwardly questions The Society is an apostate. My writing this book would be construed as apostasy by most JWs, even though I am simply telling the story of my life as I lived it and making observations of my life as a JW in the context of living it for decades.

That doesn't matter to them because if you were once a JW and you then publicly question The Society or say something unflattering about them, you are an apostate. You are not just shunned at that point, you and your entire family and friends and other associates are specifically zeroed in on with suspicion and loathing. To make this point more clear, let me share with you a story about one Watch Tower Society president in the past. This Governing Body member went so far as to publicly state that

Jehovah's Witnesses did not kill apostates <u>only because it was against the law of the countries they lived in</u>, otherwise it would be a righteous thing for them to do! Wow. This sounds exactly like other religious extremists who kill and terrorize in the name of God.

So you can see that my questioning the "generation" teaching right in the House of God in front of many Bethelites was actually a very dangerous thing to do. The young pious couple at the table end actually scolded me for asking these things. Fortunately for me, GS- was a very nice and reasonable man. He always asked our opinions on whatever we were discussing, and he didn't seem to mind my telling him exactly what was on my mind, even if it wasn't the JW robot thinking everybody expected. So, I said my piece, explaining my concerns as best I could, and as respectfully as I could, which kicked off a lively discussion at the table.

I recall that after the discussion about what I brought up died down, GS- simply looked at me, smiled, and said, "Well, you might be onto something Brock, who knows?" Those words killed the animosity that had been brewing against me at the table, at least for the time being. It didn't, however, change one single thing about how anybody at the table believed regarding the term "this generation." Neither did it cause any one of them to think Armageddon wouldn't be coming any minute now, maybe right during breakfast!

Fast forward about fifteen or so years. I would find myself reading in the latest *Watchtower* magazine almost the exact same arguments I made to GS- that day at the breakfast table on this very subject! You see, The Society had decided to redefine what "this generation" meant in the article I was reading, and they used the same reasoning I had made many years earlier with GS-. Actually, The Society has readdressed this issue in additional writings. They have since that time given more "new light" about the meaning of "this generation" as well as the timing of

Armageddon, explaining that it could be later in the future than we might think.

I guess the worm eating, face melting, head exploding day of God's vengeance will have to wait a bit longer. Go ahead and finish your breakfast.

Look, I know some will read this and say that I am mocking the Watch Tower Society and thus fulfilling the scripture that says, "Where is this promise of His coming?" Wrong. I am not mocking the idea of a return of Jesus Christ. I do believe myself that we are in fact living in "end times." Besides, Jehovah's Witnesses are not the only people who think scripture is being fulfilled and that we are living in the "last days." So, I would not mock the reasonable assumption that God would want to clean up this bad world, and perhaps soon.

Yet, "soon" is relative, especially when you are talking about the fleeting life of a human on this planet. To bring this home, I want to point out that the Watch Tower Bible and Tract Society printed an edition of the *Watchtower* magazine in the very year I had this discussion with GS- that actually said the following in big letters on its cover, "1914 - The Generation That Will Not Pass Away." On this cover, they showed pictures of a dozen and half of the better-known older Bethelites, some GB members and their wives and others who held various important positions in The Organization. This *Watchtower* magazine cover was clearly stating with absolute certainty that the end of this known world would come before these older folks would die out. Period. It was in bold letters, in pictures, and the article inside was clear about this assertion as well. Well, today as I write this story, <u>every single one of the people on that cover is dead, and they have been so for nearly two decades!</u> That magazine cover, that article and its entire premise was one hundred percent wrong and has been proven to be so beyond any doubt whatsoever. How Jehovah's Witnesses today can justify that amazing blunder is beyond me.

125

My problem was then, and still is now, the JW fixation on the destruction of everybody else but JWs. To me it is insulting, unloving, and frankly presumptuous. What is especially insulting is their trying to put dates on this Armageddon timeframe based on an always-changing calculation that has proven over and over again to be wrong. Jesus clearly said nobody would know that day or hour, yet JWs constantly declare (or imply) a new end-of-the-world date almost every other decade. This ends up ruining the lives of many people, as well as their own credibility, in the process. Deuteronomy 18:22 makes this point clear, "If what a prophet proclaims in the name of the LORD does not take place or come true, that is a message the LORD has not spoken. That prophet has spoken presumptuously. Do not be afraid of him."

You tell me, has what Jehovah's Witnesses said about all the dates they have used for over 130 years ever came true in any clearly seen, discernible, unarguable way whatsoever? JWs will try to wiggle out of this by saying, "Hey, we've never claimed to be prophets, so that scripture doesn't apply to us." Wrong. JW literature compares JWs to prophets all the time, claiming to be the Isaiah "anti-type" or the Jeremiah "class" and so on. (These are JW terms I won't explain here. Suffice it to say, they compare themselves to prophets all the time.) No, Jehovah's Witnesses act the prophet every day. Therefore, they can't have it both ways then when their prophecies go awry.

JWs acted the prophet when giving us dates like 1925. They said this date was to be "the return of Abraham" in the now infamous "Millions now living will never die" speech given in 1918 by The Society's president at that time. Humorously, all the millions who personally heard that talk, or read the book based on it, are now in fact dead. 1925 came and went, and nothing happened.

JWs acted the prophet when they foisted the date 1975 on us when the *Watchtower* magazine declared many years before 1975 that it was "The end of 6,000 years of mankind's history to begin the Sabbath-like rein of Christ to usher in the New World." Well, for people under the age of forty today in the JW faith, they should note that they are alive only because their parents didn't listen to JW advice to refrain from having children before 1975. They advised this because, after all, why would you want to "go through Armageddon" with young children? That was actual advice from my own elders, that is, avoid having children! 1975 came and went, and nothing happened.

However, even that is not enough for the JW prophets to demand from you. They then will also advise you to sell your homes, instruct you to not go to college, and tell you to not worry about retiring in this "old system of things" because of these dates. As a result, when 1914, 1925, 1975 or 1984 ticked by with unfulfilled expectations, the faithful and obedient JW remained homeless, childless, and totally unprepared financially for their future. Old age set in for these poor folks with no retirement money saved up, with no home equity, with no real means of making a decent living, and with no children to help them in their advanced age and years of need.

Such a thing is simply unacceptable and inexcusable for a religion to do to its people, over and over again, for well over 130 years and counting. Especially for a religion that declares itself to be "The Truth."

I now look back on my time with GS- at Bethel and think it's kind of funny and sad. It's funny that simple points of concern about a key religious issue ("this generation") an innocent young man had so many years ago, took an army of older men who run that religion to finally concede to. Of course, a glance at the calendar has forced their hand, hasn't it?

Apocalypse... not now.

It's sad that this same young man had to worry that his tongue would rot out of his mouth just for having legitimate questions about it that have since been proven right.

Missing meetings is wrong; unless you work for God

When I lived at God's House in the early 1980s, the average U.S. income was about $20,000 a year. In comparison to that, my first year at Bethel brought me exactly $1,859, which I laughingly filed on my income tax form that year. This was actually below the lowest poverty level wage line they had on the charts. So, in God's House, we lived poorer than the poor.

Because Bethel was a religious institution, the legal entity that controlled Bethel (the Watch Tower Bible and Tract Society) got around minimum wage laws and paid so little because they provided food, shelter, medical, dental and just about every "major expense" for us. Of course, they didn't work "minor expenses" into the calculation which were for things like personal toiletries, clothes, entertainment, food that wasn't part of the Bethel meal plan, travel, furniture, gifts, auto expenses (if you were lucky enough to have a car) and of course savings. That little stipend they gave us had to go to all those other "incidentals." Needless to say, we were always broke, and often relied on hand outs from other JWs who took pity on us.

Retirement? Well, we had no pension set up by Bethel, and of course there was no 401k plans back then that we could contribute to, not that we would have actually had any money to contribute. Retirement would simply be "the new system of things in a paradise Earth"! So, you see, if you were a Bethel "lifer," you would either work right through Armageddon, or you worked until you dropped dead, whichever came first.

Guess which came first?

Anyway, I'd like to give this some context for those who don't realize how hard the Bethel work schedule was, and probably still is, for those poor souls who worked there. I'd like for you to get an idea of how grueling the work was for the little pay we got. This was my normal work schedule assignment back then:

- Monday through Friday 8:00 AM – 5:45 PM, with a one hour lunch. (I had to walk many blocks each way just to eat my meals.)

- Saturday 8:00 AM – 12:00 PM with only one Saturday off per month.

- Walking watchman duty about every six weeks, which means after dinner you pulled a four hour stint late into the night and still had to be at breakfast the next day ready to work regardless of the watchman assignment. This was to alleviate the workload for those serving as watchmen.

- Dish duty about every other month. This was a couple-hour stint, and was also done after dinner to help alleviate the workload for those serving in the dining room.

That said, even with this intense work schedule, you were still expected to get your ten-plus hours in field service (the preaching work), and to make all of the regular meetings as well. After all, you still were a Jehovah's Witness, and this was simply a requirement of any "good" Witness. "Going to meetings" by the way, is the JW way of saying "going to church," only JWs went to five meetings a week, not one.

Too, if you "served" in the congregation, like helping with book or magazine distribution, running the audio and/or stage, etc., that was extra time put in as well. No quarter was given to accommodate that extra time for those duties; you simply had more work to do. Hence, if you "served," you showed up early or stayed late afterwards, and worked longer and harder than everybody else work, in addition to your Bethel work schedule.

Oh, and by the way, if you were a first year Bethelite, then you had to read the Bible through, cover to cover, on top of all regular "personal study" for your meetings and talk preparations, and so on. JWs give "talks" (sermons) at their meetings, which is like a pastor handing the reins over to others, like deacons, so they could give sermons too.

Finally, the first year Bethelite had one more set of special meetings and study, just for them, added to everything else outlined above! Whew!

Jehovah's Witnesses keep a very busy schedule as it is, but when you are a Bethelite, it borders on the insane, as you have very little time for yourself. I get tired just thinking about everything I did back then. I still can't believe that some Bethelites actually risked getting into trouble by working outside Bethel in what was called "G-jobs." I don't recall what the G in G-job stood for, but these G-guys actually held part time G-jobs at night or the weekends or whenever they could to make extra G-money because we were paid so G-wiz poorly. That was an example of incredible, superhuman effort if you ask me. They shouldn't have been kicked out of Bethel if their outside work activities were found out, they should have been given a G-medal.

Anyway, I was finally getting used to this intense schedule and then the Bethel powers that be dropped a bomb on us: Overtime! Yes, folks, on top of everything else, we would be doing another four hour shift Monday through Saturday after supper for as many weeks as necessary to put out a new book that was to be released at the next convention. So, for week after week, we worked twenty hours a week more than what I just outlined above. Yes, you got it. We had a least a sixty-four hour work week ahead of us, week after week. And no, we didn't get a bump in our otherwise meager "allowance" for that overtime either. Overtime was just another wonderful "privilege" in which we could take part.

Being naive at the time, I asked if I could be excused from overtime work on my meeting nights. Let me explain: growing up as a Jehovah's Witness, it was spoken from the Kingdom Hall podium and written in our *Watchtower* magazine, as well as other books we had, that for those of us that worked in regular worldly jobs, we should <u>never</u> allow these jobs to keep us from making our JW meetings. Missing meetings was very much frowned upon in the JW world, even for your work that earned you a proper living. JWs actually expected you to <u>quit your job</u> if your employer tried to force you to miss too many meetings. It was explained to us that this was to make sure you kept your spiritual health intact, which was much more important than any money you might receive from your worldly job. I grew up knowing and obeying this edict, always making sure my job never interfered with my attending meetings and even giving up good jobs if they began to get in the way of meeting attendance.

Naturally, when the Bethel bosses asked me to work overtime, I applied the same principle and asked to be excused from overtime work on my meeting nights in order to not miss my all-important meetings. Nothing doing; that request was denied. I found out that when you work for the Watch Tower Bible and Tract Society, missing JW meetings is OK. Your own personal spiritual health evidently doesn't matter at that point. There was also nobody to tell you to quit that horrible job that would force you to miss meetings, mainly because your employer is "The Watch Tower Society" itself and your "boss" is your Bethel overseer.

I found out then that the grunts that work for the Watch Tower Bible and Tract Society basically are forced into slave labor for peanuts for pay, and then forced to miss meetings on top of that! Wow, some "spiritual paradise" this turned out to be. This exploitation of the average Bethel worker is one reason why I believe Bethel goes through so many people, and why so many Bethelites return home as damaged goods. They find out that in the end, they really don't matter all that much as individuals while at God's House, and their "spiritual health" isn't a priority at all should it conflict with making books and magazines for The Society.

Eventually, I left Bethel, finished college and got a real job that lead to a real career. After much ladder climbing, I now work for one of the most influential companies in the world. This company treats me better than I ever was treated at Bethel, overtime-wise and in every other way as well. I'm given dignity, respect, and appreciation. The best part is that not only do I love my work, it provides my family a good income. On top of that, my career has given me international recognition and provided me with friends and associates who are some of the most accomplished people in the world. In contrast, Bethel works you like a dog, keeps you anonymous, makes you sacrifice in ways you are not prepared to, pays you next to nothing, has no real appreciation for you when you are there, and provided no help for you when you leave.

I say this for any of you young folks out there reading this: You don't have to work for peanuts the rest of your life just because The Society tells you making money is worldly. The truth is, many JWs are simply jealous when you do well financially; I found that out personally. These powers that be really don't care about you at all. I think most JWs find satisfaction in seeing you struggle with menial, low paying jobs like most of them do. They are like the proverbial bucket of crawdads. When you put one crawdad in a bucket, it could crawl out easily by itself. But put two or three crawdads together in a bucket, and they pull each other back down where none of them gets out.

If you don't believe me, just ask any ex-Bethelite about what a Bethel severance package looks like. Even after years of low paying, slave labor, you get nothing when you leave there except a swift kick in the pants. I got a letter that was very terse. It basically said, "Thanks for your service. Now get out and make room for the next guy." Even most so-called worldly companies have more sense to treat people better than that.

I have since stopped going to those JW meetings, but it's certainly not because of my job.

Hey, you're no Bethelite!

I need to make this clear up front: it's impossible to be a Jehovah's Witness and then to become a Bethelite, without it going to your head. I don't care who you are, it will mess with you.

When you are told all your life that Bethel is so important, so key to the spiritual life of every living Jehovah's Witness, so tied into God's will and essential for the salvation of the entire human race, well, how could that not change the way you looked at yourself? This is especially true when the JW pecking order is demonstrated to you repeatedly through the daily life of simply living as a Jehovah's Witness. How could a twenty-something kid newly arriving at Bethel not think of himself as more important than before, and not consider himself more entitled?

I'm telling you, it's impossible.

That didn't mean that we had to be jerks about it though. We Bethelites were instructed to take our assignment with humility. We were told that to us "much was given" so therefore "much was expected." (Luke 12:48) This "much" that was expected evidently meant mind numbing and unending hard work, and as I said before, it also meant that we were expected to take our "privilege" with humility. I never quite figured out what the "much given" part was, because I never felt I was given much of anything at all. To me, Bethel only took. I once described Bethel life to another newly arriving Bethelite this way: Life at Bethel was like you unselfishly offering a friend a bite of your newly opened candy bar, only to have that friend proceed to eat the whole thing leaving you with a little sliver. That's what Bethel did to my life: it took everything and left nothing but a sliver for me.

Anyway, it was amusing to see some guys go against their natural inclination to actually try to be humble after becoming a Bethelite. Since it wasn't really in their nature to be that way, they did this competitively. These guys would often try to "out humble" each other! Can you imagine that? "I'm more humble than you are!" "No. I'm the humblest of all!"

Well, I wasn't any different from most new Bethelites in that regard. Even before I went to Bethel, it already started to go to my head. For example, immediately after I was accepted to Bethel, but before I actually went there, I was a hero in my home congregation. People I knew all my life started asking for my perspective on things that I had no clue about, as if I suddenly had a direct channel to The Society. It's weird that grown men and women who otherwise took me for granted as just another kid all the years they knew me, suddenly started treating me like their Circuit or District Overseers whom they revered. I wasn't sure how to deal with that.

This was also the case while I was at Bethel. When I visited a congregation that normally did not have Bethelites around, I would be treated special. For example, older sisters in the congregation would make a beeline for me and in the ensuing conversation slyly introduce their daughters to me. This happened to me more than once. This never happened to me before I was a Bethelite. In my pre-Bethel years, I had to get around otherwise cautious mothers to hunt down their daughters on my own.

Interestingly though, I found out that at the Bethel location itself, I was the same nobody I was before I was selected to go there. You see, there were hundreds like me there, thousands actually. So I was a Bethelite? Big deal, so was that guy, that guy, that guy, and that guy. At Bethel itself, I never felt special as a Bethelite. Yet, whenever I left and went some place where there were not any other Bethelites, well, then I got all that extra attention.

So, I lived this strange world of the dichotomy of a Bethelite: The JW nobody / The JW rock star.

This turned out to be a very difficult thing to navigate at times. For me, being a Bethelite ended up in the long run to be more of a burden than a benefit. Let me give you a few examples of that.

☆

Once, my friend asked me to go to a party with him that was a long way from Bethel, somewhere deep in New Jersey. He said it was going to be a big party, and no other Bethelites would be there. Of this he was sure. That was code-speak meaning that we would get lots of attention from girls at this party and not have to compete with other Bethelites for it. It also turned out that this was a costume party, so we had to make up some costumes for it. Keep in mind that since all Bethelites are broke, how would we make up a good costume with no money? The simple answer: The "hopper room"!

Hoppers were places located everywhere in Bethel where you put clothes and other items you didn't want, but thought other Bethelites might need. Also, many JWs who visited Bethel donated clothing and other items to the hoppers as well. All of the individual hoppers were gathered from on a regular basis, and the items from these hoppers eventually filled one large room we called the hopper room. This hopper room was a lot like a Salvation Army or Goodwill store, but everything there was free for us Bethelites. Most Bethelites at some time or another rummaged through the individual hoppers, or the large hopper room, doing what we called "hopper shopping."

For example, I needed the hopper room when I was new to Bethel because I found out I didn't have enough warm clothes to get me through the harsh New York winters. The clothes in the hopper room were by and large hideous, so I used that hopper room very sparingly for my actual wardrobe. Although I was broke, I wasn't desperate. And after all, you weren't going to find a cool new Members Only jacket in there, that was for sure.

Hey, you're no Bethelite!

Still, it was a great place to create a costume. So, as what should we go dressed? Well, both of us wanted to make sure we showed off our bodies as much as possible because we thought that would attract girls. After looking through the hopper room for ideas, we decided to dress up as roguish pirates.

You see, we found boots that must have been from a larger woman because they fit us perfectly, and went up to our knees just like a pirate's boots should. We found scarves that looked great as pirate headbands. We found unused eye liner that we used to draw skulls and crossbones and anchors on our biceps. We found puffy shirts (actually blouses) which looked like, well, pirate shirts that showed off our chests nicely. We found puffy pants too, that we ripped and tore to look more rough-and-tumble and pirate-ish when we tucked them into our boots. We rolled up our shirt (blouse) sleeves to show off our arms, and then tied more scarves around our arms to create bicep bands. "This was awesome," we thought. "Perfect pirates. The best sexy pirates ever!"

So, off we went, thinking that we were going to be the life of the party. When we got to the party, we were a hit with the chicks, which had been our main goal. They ooh-ed and aah-ed over our costumes, grabbed our arms, and so on. Nice!

Unfortunately, we miscalculated how the chaperones at the party would receive us. You see, many of the older sisters there were offended by our costumes. For starters, they didn't think being a pirate, someone who pillaged and raped, befitted a Christian at all, let alone a Bethelite who should know better than to emulate that kind of character. That was strike one. We also displayed too much of our bodies, which showed an immodesty unsuitable for any true Christian. That was strike two. The last straw was that we were mainly wearing women's clothes, what with the blouses, women's boots, women's scarves, mascara, and so on. Strike three. We were out.

We were summarily reprimanded by these indignant sisters with these simple words, "You're no Bethelites."

★

Once we had another party to go to near Fire Island. I couldn't wait for this one. This place was also well away from Bethel and we heard it was going to be a big party with rich JW girls there who were hot and worldly. We heard they flirted wildly, dressed seductively, and would easily let you make out with them. Best yet, they would never tell on you and get you into any sort of trouble, because that is not the way they did things. Normal Witness girls could make trouble for you if they actually fell in love and wanted to marry. You know, all that mushy stuff. The girls on Fire Island just wanted to party. These parties and the girls who went to them were influenced by the many bikini movies that were coming out in the early 1980s, movies like *Spring Break* and *Hardbodies*.

We thought, "Oh boy!" After being cooped up at Bethel and not touching a girl for quite a long time, we were up to seeing what this kind of party was all about.

After a very long, expensive and arduous journey (the details of which I will leave out here) we finally got to the party. Suffice it to say, I was getting edgy during the trip. I so wanted to get to this darn party, but we were going to be very late arriving there because of many false starts and diversions. I kept hopeful because I figured the trip would be worth it once I met all these hot chicks who would certainly want me over all the other dudes there. After all, I was a Bethelite.

Well, when we finally got there, the party was in full swing. In fact, it was in such full swing that most of the girls there had already pretty much paired up with the guys they wanted to be with. It was beginning to dawn on me that our entrance was met with exactly zero fanfare. This was the opposite of what I was expecting. We sat there like idiots long enough to figure out that in order to get some attention, we had to take matters into our own hands, just like "regular" Witness guys had to do.

So I circled the area and found a prospect who didn't seem to be otherwise engaged. She was extremely hot, just like I heard the girls at this party would be. Since it was a beach setting, these girls dressed very skimpily. I had not seen a chick in a bikini top for Lord knew how long. It was very exciting to meet hot girls in flimsy bikinis that, per the 1980s singer Cindi Lauper, "just wanna have fun."

I approached the girl and revved up my game. It was going pretty good, and we even danced together. I was dressed skimpily myself and was drinking booze like everybody else. I even started using tough and salty language like everyone else too. Hey, when in Rome...

The girl seemed to be interested in me and I thought I hit the jackpot because it was looking like I had this girl where I wanted her and we'd be making out soon. But then I made a big mistake. I thought I'd "seal the deal" with her and told her I was a Bethelite, which I thought would be something in my favor. Nope. It had the exact opposite effect. She accused me of lying to try to impress her. I insisted to her that I was in fact straight from Bethel. She didn't believe me. She said I didn't look like a Bethelite, and I didn't dress like a Bethelite, and I certainly did not act like a Bethelite. "Besides, no Bethelite would come to this party," she said. I brought my friend over to support my claim. This just made it worse because then she actually did believe that I was from Bethel, and was then even more turned off by that fact.

In the end, it turned out that this very worldly Witness girl, who liked to party, drink and carouse while dressed in next to nothing, suddenly became judgmental of me because I acted in the same way as she and her friends did. To her mind, I should have known better than to be at this party since I carried a higher title than the rest of the people there. Her response to me was a perfect example of what all Jehovah's Witnesses do best: judge each other. Ironically, even Witness girls like this did that kind of judging.

She left me, disappointed, declaring her final edict, "You're no Bethelite."

If it walks like a duck... then you're a brief wearing fairy

As a young man in God's House, I was in pretty good shape. To give this story context as well as to admit my own faults up front, I will tell you this: I was a vain young man who worked out quite a bit. I had a good body and I knew it. I hung around other brothers like me and we all wore clothes that showed off our "guns" and "six packs" as much as a Bethelite was allowed to. We all probably laughed a bit too loud together and had a bit too much fun wearing our '80s muscle shirts, and we probably got just a bit too much attention from the girls. (That is, at least as far as some important Bethel leaders were concerned.) In time, I found out that this alone would mean I would never really get anywhere in the Bethel world. But, I was clueless about it at the time, being a young, dumb kid.

I worked in the factory making Bible literature and shared a locker room with a Bethel overseer who I'll call RW. This guy was one of my least favorite Bethel people. He was a short, pudgy, funny looking man around forty years of age with a big bottom lip. He had a Napoleon complex, lofty eyes and a chip on his shoulder bigger than he was. You could just smell the haughtiness emanating from him. Not all brothers with "power" at Bethel were like him, as even most of the odd ones had some niceness about them. Not this guy. They called people like this a "Bethel Heavy" to indicate the weight of their importance. However, in his case it also happened to describe his fat ass, as well as the heft of his homely wife.

Now, as background to this story, you should know that whenever the issue of somebody's sexual orientation came up (like with Michael Jackson for example) the Bethel mantra was, "If it walks like a duck and it quacks like a duck, it's a duck." The meaning was simple: If a man looked or acted effeminate, then he was gay. Why talk about it any further? Enough said. Case closed. Discussion over.

142

Another thing I want to explain is that at that time there were large billboards all over town with a male model wearing only skimpy briefs. It caused much stir in Bethel for being very provocative. The women secretly loved this billboard because the model was well built, and the bulge in his briefs was prominently displayed as he lounged for the picture. The jealous Bethel men simply dismissed this billboard guy as "gay" because, after all, male models are all gay, aren't they? Enough said. Case closed. Discussion over. (I later found out to my amusement that this model was not gay.)

A final thing you need to know is that I wore colored briefs, very similar to the one the model wore on that billboard. Yet, nobody saw me in that underwear, except my roommates and the guys in my locker room. The reason I wore them will become evident in my story.

Now that you have the necessary background, I can get to my main story. I was changing into my work clothes in the locker room one day, and we guys were cutting up like we usually did. It was a locker room after all, so there was lots of trash talking, lots of teasing, lots of "capping" on each other, towel snapping, and so on. We were young and full of it, and we did what young guys do. However, there were limits to what kind of capping you could do. For example, somebody's wife was out of bounds to tease about. As was their mother. We never teased about serious things like if somebody was sick or hurt. So, even though we were dumb kids, we had the sense to limit our teasing to a reasonable degree.

RW was the top dog in that locker room, as well as being the oldest and having the highest title. If he "capped" on you, you laughed and didn't dare say anything back. You stayed capped, and thought it a compliment that he would even talk to you. We had heard numerous stories of people who went up against RW, and they usually ended up leaving Bethel soon after. This wasn't going to happen to us, we told ourselves. So, we always gave RW the respect he demanded.

Well, this particular day, RW zeroed in on me. He looked at me with everyone listening and said quite loudly:

RW: Hey Brock. I was driving and saw that billboard today with your "boy" on it. How is he doing? You guys get together yet? [we all knew which billboard he was talking about.]

Locker room: OOOOOOOOOOH

Me: Where did that come from? Why would you say something like that to me?

RW: Well, you both wear the same underwear, so I thought you "knew" each other. [snicker]

Locker room: OOOOOOOOOOH, SNAAAAAP!!!!

Me: [incredulous, sputtering] ww...what? Are you trying to say I'm gay?

RW: Well, if it walks like a duck, and talks like a duck... [snicker]

Locker room: HaHa Ha HaHa HaHa HaHa HaHa Ha Ha Ha Ha HaHaHa HaHaHaHaHaHa HaHaHaHa

Me: [very hurt - voice raised] You are way out of line! You have no right to accuse me of something like that in front of my friends. You're just jealous because you couldn't wear the underwear I do. You couldn't squeeze your fat butt into them, and if you did, you'd look like a little stuffed sausage!

Locker room: OHHHHHHHHHHHHHHHHHHHHH. HaHaHaHa.

RW: [red-faced, very angry, pointing at me] OUTSIDE, NOW!

The guys all looked at me with a "bye, nice knowing you" look as we marched out of the locker room together. With a good distance between us and the locker room, RW turned and started in on me:

RW: How DARE you speak to me that way...

Me: [cutting him off] HOW DARE I? HOW DARE YOU! You cannot sit there as the older man among us and accuse me of homosexuality in front of all my friends like that. That was extremely humiliating, and I won't take that kind of crap from anyone, not you, no one. I didn't volunteer to come here to be abused by the likes of you. Just last week you were hinting around that I liked the ladies "a bit too much," and now you're going the opposite way and hinting I like men a little too much. Why are you so fixated on my sexuality?

RW: [a little sheepish now] Look, I was just trying to counsel you. Back in my day, if an older brother gave a simple hint, I took it as a command. I had said something about that underwear you wear before this, and you didn't take the hint. So I was trying again.

Me: You're kidding right? You really don't like my underwear? Look, I wear these mainly because they give me support, OK? I don't like boxers for that reason.

RW: Well, you can wear the kind I wear then.

Me: I don't like those "tighty whities" either. They show stains too easily and the laundry room boils and bleaches white underwear so they wear out very fast. I don't want to have to rinse them before putting them in the laundry and then get them back with bleach holes eaten into them after a few weeks. These colored briefs don't have any of those problems... as if it were any of your business.

RW: Well, to me, they just look like what guy's like that gay male model wears, and that doesn't speak well for a Christian man.

Me: First of all, nobody but my locker room brothers and my roommates see my underwear. So, exactly who is this "not speaking well to"? It's not like worldly people see me in them. Second of all, that male model happens to be married and jealous people like you only label him as gay because you can't stand his good looks, which is typical of funny looking Witnesses with any sort of power. Also, you don't seem to have a problem with Brother Tim. He wears the exact same underwear as I do, and you've never said a word to Tim about it at all, nothing.

RW: Yes, I know, but Tim doesn't fixate on his body like you do, and he is very frail, and besides, he's a quiet man. You, well, you're all pumped up and... well, you just look like those... you know... male model guys to me.

Me: So, you are saying you just don't like this underwear on me then, right? If I'm in shape, and actually look good in these underwear, that is where the "not speaking well for a Christian man" part comes in? You only like it when a guy is skinny and quiet and doesn't threaten you? Then he could wear women's underwear if he wanted and you would have no problem with it? This sounds like a personal problem on your part, not mine. Jealousy doesn't suit an older man like you.

RW: Well, what would Brother Gangas say about all this? You're speaking to me this way? [RW knew I was pretty close to this Governing Body member]

Me: I'm glad you brought that up. Brother Gangas is more mature than that to care what a young Bethelite's underwear looks like. He definitely wouldn't be jealous of my body like you apparently are. Let's go ask him.

RW: [silence, thinking out his next move...]

Me: Look, if you don't want me to wear them because it really bothers you for whatever reason, and you're that adamant about it, why not just pull me aside and speak to me as a brother? Why not just ask me? I would get rid of these things and wear something else if it truly offends you and you were to ask as my brother. Ask in a mature way, one-on-one, and I'll deal with it. But don't try to humiliate and bully me like that in front of others - that just will not work on me.

RW: [coldly] Do what you want.

Me: Ask me as a brother...

RW: [walking away...] Do what you want.

By then the guys had left the locker room to start their work. I finished changing and went to my station. Everybody looked at me, but nobody said anything at first. At the next break, I told my story and they all were amazed I wasn't kicked out of Bethel for saying what I said to him, both in the locker room and in private later. Yet, there I was, still in Bethel. I had gone up against the big bad RW and lived to tell about it.

Of course, I never got an apology from this little troll of a man, not even a personal one, let alone a public one. Of course, he wouldn't actually humble himself and ask me as a brother to stop doing the thing he claimed bothered him so much. No, this was about jealousy, power, control, and ego. Pure and simple.

After a week or so, I realized RW couldn't touch me. The way he looked at me after that caused it to slowly dawn on me that I actually had something on him now. I think he thought long and hard how bad he'd look for saying what he said to me if we did go to another more mature and more powerful brother about this. However, I also knew that after that, he had his eye on me, always looking for just one mistake...

By this time, my journey had slowed and my idealism diminished, considerably. The hope of finding the spiritual paradise, the place where God lives, began to fade.

Fast forward to today. My body has since aged, gotten a bit thicker and sagged some, and is certainly not as good as shape as it was back then. Guess what kind of underwear I still sport though? At least my wife thinks they look good, and she's now the only one who sees me in them.

We're also the only two people on the planet who care about it one way or the other.

Welcome to New York, now f**k off

When you were new to God's House, they called you a "new boy." That term, though accurate, was really a slur to those of us getting used to Bethel life. So, when you did something particularly stupid, like putting your clothes in the weekly laundry bag incorrectly, you were hit with a dismissive, "Pshhh. Such a new boy." Long time Bethelites had little use for us new boys as we were mostly just a nuisance to them with all of our stupid questions and aggravating mistakes. When they weren't telling us what to do, they were ignoring us altogether. I never could tell which was worse.

It turned out that I was a neophyte to New York City as well. The city also took some getting used to. I mean, have you ever actually <u>seen</u> the subway maps of New York City? Have you tried to figure out how to get somewhere catching the local and the express, uptown and cross-town and such? Well, it was tough to learn.

It was also tough to see how some of the less fortunate lived in the city. I once took the train to the Bronx Zoo with some friends. The ride felt like going to the end of the world. At one point, the subway came above ground, and we eventually passed through the South Bronx area, which looked like a war zone. That area was filled with burned out buildings, burned out cars, and burned out people. It was the summer time when I went, so the people I witnessed from that elevated train just hung out of the burned out windows trying to get cool. They stood on burned out fire escapes with nothing much to do but look pitiful. The look on the people's faces of utter despair was heartbreaking. I was so inexperienced in life that I actually cried at seeing this.

By the time I got to the Zoo, I was emotionally spent. I had to gather myself in order to try to have a nice day. Once we made it into the Zoo, it became a strange oasis in an otherwise bleak world. I didn't look out the window on the ride back home that evening.

☆

On one of my first free Saturdays off, I started walking right out of my front door from the Brooklyn Heights where I lived, just to see the sights. I kept walking and walking because it was such a beautiful day. I walked up and I walked down, not really keeping track of where I was. As I grew tired, I looked around and realized that the neighborhood had changed quite a bit. The place was a bit scary looking where I ended up. I went into a store to ask for directions so I could find my way back home. The store was pretty much empty except for the few guys who were hanging out there. They just looked at me like I was an idiot, which I was. You see, I had stumbled into Bedford Stuyvesant, one of the worst neighborhoods in New York at that time. It appeared that I had stumbled into a "front" of some sort, maybe for drugs or gambling or something worse. What a dummy I was! Billy Joel sang about this area in his recently released song *You may be right (I may be crazy),* and one of the things he says he did in that song that demonstrated his craziness was, "I walked through Bedford Stuy alone." Well, I have to say, Billy only sang about it. I actually did it. I got myself out of there quickly, and hoofed it back as fast as I could with the hope that I could make it home before the sun went down. I quickly realized that I could use the relatively new World Trade Center's "Twin Towers" as a landmark to get me back home. It would be decades later that on TV I would see these same towers fall during the infamous attacks on September 11th, 2001.

☆

Another strange thing happened to me in Manhattan one day, right by the Guggenheim Museum. My friends were on the museum side of Fifth Avenue, and for some reason, I had crossed the street to the Central Park side. I think I was getting a pretzel or something. Well, a parade started to come down the street and I began to watch it with great curiosity, separated from my friends. As the parade came down Fifth Avenue, I realized it was a Gay Pride Parade. Now keep in mind, JWs are especially repulsed by this particular sexual sin. Also, I was pretty sheltered in life as I had never really seen a homosexual before, or if I had, I didn't know it. So, this was all new to me.

I can tell you that a Gay Pride Parade was not the best place for a young impressionable Jehovah's Witness boy to see gays for the first time. Remember, this was the early 1980s and homosexuality was not all that much in the open for the most part, except for in the biggest of cities, and even then only in certain places in those cities. I watched with amazement at first as the parade of guys wearing only G-strings or chaps with the buttocks cut out went by me. I watched in shock as guys came by and started saying things to me like, "Hey sugar, you want some of daddy?" while they stuck their tongues out and flicked them at me. They then kissed each other and groped each other, laughing at my obvious shock. I actually started to cry at this, but I got hold of myself so I wouldn't be shamed in front of my friends. Fortunately, my friends were on the other side of the street not seeing my embarrassing reaction to all this.

★

The Big Apple wasn't all bad though. I saw things there that I hadn't seen before, good things too. I often found it exciting, exhilarating even. For example, I had always loved architecture, especially big buildings, so being right across from the Twin Towers every day and visiting the Empire State Building, the Chrysler Building, the Citigroup Building and others, was a very cool thing for me. I also visited most of the New York iconic locations like Times Square, Grand Central Station, the Statue of Liberty, the Brooklyn Bridge, Central Park, Rockefeller Center, and so on. These famous places were part of our national lexicon, awesome to experience firsthand and easy to love.

What wasn't so easy to love was the native New Yorker. The New York no-nonsense attitude displayed by the locals became part of my Bethel experience and adjustment. Whether worldly or Witness, these people were just more "in your face" than what I was used to. Now, I realize that some New Yorkers will be reading this story, so I apologize up front if I hurt your feelings here. I am simply stating the way I felt back then. Besides, let's be real, this can't be the first time you've heard this.

Let me give you an example of what I mean. I told a native New York Bethelite, relatively early in my stay, where I was from. He responded, "Boy. That's too bad," and he meant it! That really hurt my feelings. Up until then, I thought my hometown was a desirable place to come from. This guy made me feel like crap for being from there. Also, while out in the preaching work, I experienced rejection on a whole new level in New York City which was more intense and colorful than I ever had back home. Another thing was that I had never been scared of homeless people before until I went to New York. Until then, most homeless people I had encountered were just pitiful and helpless looking. In New York, however, they were aggressive and frightening. In the city, store owners barked at me, cab drivers growled at me, people on the street never said "hi," and so on. The bottom line: it was tough for me to get used to living in New York City.

My feelings about this were further supported when I met a brother who was from the South who was also new to Bethel. I liked this guy and confided my feelings about New Yorkers to him. He responded by telling me a story I will relate here:

Brother Southerner says, "I was talkin' to somebody in my nyew congreshun and a local brother there was makin' fun of me. He says to me he says: 'Hey brother, yew syure talk funny, I caint understand yew. Hawh hawh'." Brother Southerner continued, "So I says to him I says, well, I s'pose it's 'cause I use words yewall don't hear all that often in Nyeew York City. Yew know, words like 'thank yew', 'please', 'scuse me' and such."

I thought that was hilarious.

It wasn't that I didn't find some New Yorkers just as warm as anybody else once I got to know them; it's just that most of them seemed to me to have a hard outer shell that was tough to get through at first. So, for good or for bad, right or wrong, that was the conclusion I drew. It also sets up the story I want to tell next.

One day I had a visitor come to Bethel; I was excited about this because this was rare for me due to the fact that my family never visited me all the years I was at Bethel. When most Bethelites had visitors, they felt compelled to show them around Bethel, and if possible, take them out to the city to see some sights too. Besides, we Bethelites were always hopeful our visitors would feed us somewhere. So, I took my friend into the city. We were out and about, I think around 42nd street, and we were totally acting like tourists. We grabbed a giant bagel in a local shop and marveled at its size while we chowed down on it. (New York bagels were a good value for us Bethelites because they were a lot of food for little money.) My friend and I stood staring up at the Empire State Building, probably talking a bit too loud. Then, we were stopped at a corner and I was telling the brother about the taxi cab drivers. I was saying, probably quite loudly, "New York people are rude, but the taxi cab drivers were the most rude of all. They'll run you over if you give them the chance and then flip you off and yell at you for your trouble." I said this because a cab had brushed pretty close to my friend, and I had just pulled him back out of the street, out of harm's way.

Now, the irony of this doesn't escape me today, that is, I was being rude myself by loudly accusing others of being rude. Such is as it was. Unfortunately for me that day, a little old lady had been listening to me who was obviously from New York City. She looked at me in anger, waved her umbrella at me and said, "We are not at all like that you a**hole! If you don't like it here, then why don't you f*****g go back to where you came from you [racial epithet]!"

She hobbled on in a huff. My friend and I looked at each other and then burst into laughter.

When we finally stopped laughing, I wiped away a tear and still smiling said to him, "...and I rest my case."

Mr. Coffee, you're no Joe DiMaggio

Jehovah's Witnesses are largely devoid of what most people would call heroes. Ask anyone who their hero is and you will get many different answers, some may be related to sports or politics, some may be a religious figure, or some even a family member. Almost everyone will say they have a hero.

Not Jehovah's Witnesses. We were taught that only Jesus Christ was to be our hero. Anything else would be "worshipping the creation rather than the creator." Oddly, JWs also believe that Jesus Christ is a creation of Jehovah. So that means worshiping that particular creation is acceptable. Hmmm.

As a result of this hero-phobia that Witnesses had, I didn't grow up having any sports heroes. Even though I played soccer as a young kid and would dream of being like Pele, flipping head over heels to kick the winning goal, I nevertheless made sure to avoid saying he was my hero. I also never had a poster of anybody in my room either. Posters of sports "idols" were considered "idolatry" by Jehovah's Witnesses. Also, I never even had that famous poster of Farrah Fawcett in her red bathing suit that every worldly boy had back in those days. Looking back on it, I realize now that the poster was really just a picture of teeth, hair, and nipples, since that's all we saw when we ogled it.

Posters of scantily clad girls were particularly frowned upon for young Witness boys. The most obvious reason, of course, was that these served as masturbatory vehicles. Besides, that was "worship of the creation" again, right? Now, I don't know about you, but I personally think the human female body is one of God's crowning achievements, deserving of at least some awe. It's no wonder He had to rest after He made Eve; even God knew it would be difficult to top that spectacular feat of engineering.

Regarding sports, particularly baseball, I should remind you that Pete Rose was still a hero back then in the early 1980s. He was more so than say, Joe DiMaggio, who was mostly a hero from my father's generation. Still, when it came time to hawk the ever increasingly popular coffee maker called "Mr. Coffee," well, they chose Joe over Pete to do those commercials. In my day, those Mr. Coffee commercials were kind of cool. Maybe it was a good move of the Mr. Coffee manufacturers to choose Joe DiMaggio for their salesman, I mean, in light of what happened to Pete Rose later. Joe is still a hero to many, while Pete, not so much. Heroes do come and go after all. If you don't believe me, ask O.J. Simpson

Speaking of Mr. Coffee, Bethel had its own Mr. Coffee, which was the name we gave to one of our more colorful Brooklyn denizens. We called him Mr. Coffee because he often yelled at us Bethelites for drinking coffee, which he thought was as much a drug as any other. It turns out Mr. Coffee was a New York native who had been disfellowshipped for smoking, but never made the effort to come back to the Jehovah's Witness organization after that.

You see, if you were DF'd as a JW, you could in fact be reinstated as a JW in good standing. All you had to do was slip into the Kingdom Hall for each public meeting and sit in the back and listen for about six to nine months. You would come in late and leave early to the meetings, which showed proper politeness in not making other people uncomfortable with your shameful DF'd situation. Then, after enough time passed (up to maybe even a year if your sin was especially egregious), your congregation elders would approach you and ask you if you were still doing the thing that got you DF'd in the first place. If you said "no," and also said enough times and with enough conviction that you were very sorry, and would not do that bad thing again, well, they would reinstate you! Now, your own mom and dad could talk to you again! Now, it wouldn't be so awkward at work every day if you happened to work with other JWs. Now, you could spend your weekends again knocking on the doors of strangers asking for small change for *Watchtower* and *Awake* magazines to cover the cost of printing them. Oh happy days!

Well, Mr. Coffee never bothered with all that. He was DF'd because JWs believe smoking to be a particular evil sin that requires DF'ing, what with smoking being an unclean drug and all. (So, put that in your pipe and smoke it!) Mr. Coffee thought that the issue should be a personal choice. He thought it particularly hypocritical that other drugs were OK'ed by The Society, like alcohol for example, but his particular vice was deemed a sin worthy of expulsion. His special pet peeve though, was with caffeine. He argued that drinking coffee was the same as smoking a cigarette or cigar. He argued that people got "hooked" on coffee and caused themselves health problems due to this habit just as much as anybody who smoked. Mormons in fact make this same argument, and are particularly consistent with the "drug" issue of caffeine, alcohol and tobacco, all of which they shun. Even many Southern Baptists and Seventh-day Adventists shun alcohol for this same reason. It is odd then that Jehovah's Witnesses are not holier than Mormons regarding this issue, and darn it, we were usually the most pious religion of all! What gives? Why couldn't we be as consistently more holy than all those other people?

Anyway, now that Mr. Coffee was no longer a JW in good standing, he made his arguments regarding coffee and drugs by standing in front of the 124 Columbia Heights building, every day, for hours on end, YELLING ABOUT IT AT THE TOP OF HIS LUNGS! Yes, Mr. Coffee was a little extreme on how he made his point. Since the main thrust of his objection to The Society was about coffee, he would see us coming out of the Bethel buildings, point at us and yell things like:

"Hey, Watch Tower slave! Have your fix this morning did you?!"

"Hey, you. Bethel grunt! Get your coffee fix today?!"

Sometimes he got more personal about our appearance and would take particular shots at the sisters in Bethel if he thought they were dressed provocatively, or wore too much makeup. He thought all good Christians should dress modestly and especially not wear makeup or the color red. So, he'd say things like:

"Hey you, Bethel whore! Yes, you! Dressed like a harlot today are we?"

"Hey painted hussy! Walking the streets today are you?"

By the way, there were other colorful characters in our neighborhood who hung around the Bethel buildings. One guy we nicknamed Jeremiah Johnson. He was a relatively young muscular street person who often went without a shirt in the summer time, and who had, in his own strange dirty straggly way, the rugged good looks of the western movie character we nicknamed him after. For some reason, he wanted to live in a cardboard box on the sidewalk in the front of various Bethel buildings, moving around from time to time. He was harmless for the most part, except for the occasional ranting and raving outbursts he would make from time to time, directed at no one in particular. Sometimes it seemed that he was ranting and raving at God Himself, but I never got close enough to him to try to figure out what his particular beef was. I recall that I was once woken up in the middle of the night to hear him screaming out to God about something or other.

The strange thing about Jeremiah Johnson was that every so often a big nice car would pull up to his cardboard box, pick him up and take him away. He would always return after that, cleaned up with new clothes, a new haircut, and looking and smelling much better. But the new and improved Jeremiah Johnson did not last. Rumor had it that he was the son of a rich man, dying of a venereal disease, and slowly going crazy. His wealthy father let him stay in the cardboard box, but then came and helped him out from time to time. Sometimes I found myself wishing that big car would come and get me.

Anyway, unlike the young Jeremiah Johnson, Mr. Coffee was an older man, far past middle age, and since he left the streets in the evenings, we assumed he had his own home nearby. He just did his own form of preaching like JWs did. Unfortunately for us, it took place in front of our very own Bethel buildings every day and was directed specifically against us. Because he spoke against The Society and had once been a Jehovah's Witness, we called him an apostate. Well, Mr. Coffee was a full-time apostate, I can tell you that. Had he been a JW in good standing, he would have been a pioneer due to all the time he put in to giving us a hard time.

Alas, it wasn't meant to be, as Mr. Coffee liked that smoking habit too much. Had his vice been guzzling too much beer, or maybe slurping down cases of soda, or gulping pots of coffee, well, that would have been OK. He could have even been an elder in a Witness congregation with those vices. But no. His fate would be that of a smoking full-time anti-JW apostate, rather than a booze guzzling, coffee slurping, pioneering JW elder.

As I said before, since he mostly yelled about the coffee thing, we nicknamed him Mr. Coffee. We thought this was clever because it was also making a funny reference to the famous machine that Joe DiMaggio sold on TV at that time. Mr. Coffee annoyed the locals (the non-Bethelites) in the neighborhood to no end as well. I think they actually hated this guy more than we did. He would get into altercations with them from time to time, and we heard of numerous stories about him being pushed or punched by locals there because, well, he was obnoxious. We found these stories humorous because we wanted to punch him ourselves, but of course, we didn't dare.

But by and large, the funniest story about Mr. Coffee was him being run over by a Bethelite in a truck The Society owned. How that Bethelite could miss him was a mystery to me, as the guy was larger than life and ever present. But that's how the story was told; the Bethelite simply didn't see Mr. Coffee and ran him over. It turned out in the end that Mr. Coffee required medical care, but wasn't too seriously injured. With this incident though, he now had even more fodder for hating The Society and for despising all Witnesses in general.

By the way, as we did everything else, we eventually nicknamed the truck that ran over Mr. Coffee.

We called it "The Coffee Creamer."

You can lead an elder to college, but you can't make him think

After a long stint in God's House, I finally took my first vacation and couldn't wait to see everybody back home again. In Bethel, you don't get a whole lot of vacation time. I don't remember exactly how much it was (maybe two weeks per year?) but it wasn't enough. Given that Bethel doesn't give any national or personal holidays off, doesn't have a sick day policy, and requires that you work a complete year before you can use the vacation time you earned, it was meager time off. If you compared it to just about any other "worldly" job, the Bethel vacation time off policy was pretty darn pitiful.

Still, I had finally earned my time off, and got the money together to get my ticket home. I was jazzed. However, by then one of the things that hit me hard was that I was working as a "flunky" at the factory. One worldly person once called me that to my face: "Flunky." Ouch. I had never flunked anything in my life. Yet here I was labeled that by another person, just because I wanted to do something I thought was noble, because I wanted to do "God's work." Oh well. I realized that sooner or later, I was going to get a college education and get a real job so I wouldn't be a flunky anymore.

As it turns out, there was an elder in my congregation that I had grown up with, one that my family and I counted as a "family friend," who had gone to college himself. In fact, not only was he a college educated man, he was a college professor! Who could be better to ask for advice on what college to attend, what college life was like, and how to go about getting a college education? I thought I'd bring up the issue of college to him once I was back home visiting and attending a meeting there, since he had all the inside information due to the fact that he was at college every single day teaching there. I figured that now that I had pioneered and was at Bethel, I had paid my Christian dues. Certainly he

161

would see that it would be OK for me to do the same thing as he had done: go to college, get a degree, get a white-collar job earning good money, and buy a big house in which to raise a family.

Since he was a minority and a foreigner with an accent, I thought that he would understand the value of education in order to make a dollar in the good old U.S. of A. He was short, funny looking, and had a badly pockmarked face, yet he still had a pretty decent looking wife (well, for him anyway). I was sure he would be on my side, especially since we were both minorities. After all, it was conventional wisdom the reason he had his white "trophy" wife in the first place was because he had a fairly prestigious job, a few bucks in the bank, and a decent house for her to decorate and entertain in. It wasn't his rakish good looks, that was for sure.

I approached Elder Pockface at an opportune time and mentioned my goals to him. To my surprise, he told me he didn't recommend me pursuing a college education at all. He said that he supported The Society's "counsel" that worldly education and other similar selfish pursuits were not in the best interest of Christians. He also echoed the basic JW thinking that college was a worldly environment, one that taught atheistic things like evolution that would ruin you spiritually with its liberal godlessness.

Basically, he didn't want to help me at all. He actually seemed put-off by my just asking him about college. I was dumbfounded. Didn't he see the duplicity in this, being that he himself was a college professor? The rest of the conversation went something like this:

Me: [pleading voice] I can't <u>believe</u> you, Brother Pockface. You, of all people, a college professor no less, are discouraging <u>me</u> from going to college?

Pockface: [in a serious tone] Look, it's a bad, worldly environment to put yourself in, and besides, worldly pursuits like that only hinder your spiritual progress.

Me: So what am I supposed to do the rest of my life, work in a factory? I was valedictorian of my high school class and accepted to various universities with honors. But now that I've gone to Bethel, I'm supposed to forget about that?

Pockface: I know you are a smart young man, but trust me, you don't want to go to college and inundate yourself into that environment. You're doing fine now on a good spiritual path, why ruin it?

Me: Sorry, but I think that is patently hypocritical of you to say that since you went to college yourself. On top of that, you still teach at a college.

Pockface: Well, I went to college before I knew The Truth, so that is different.

Me: I don't get it, how is that different?

Pockface: Well, I didn't know any better then. I was worldly then. So, I did what worldly people do.

Me: But, you still benefit from having done it! Also, you still support the concept of college by teaching at one for heaven's sake! So, you would teach worldly people how to "get ahead," but not your own brothers?

Pockface: It's not that. College just isn't for true Christians. I have to do this; it is my profession. I've spent too long doing this in my life to simply give it up now. But you should know better.

Me: [sarcastically] So, if you would have sold drugs or ran a prostitution ring before learning The Truth, then you would still be doing that anyway? I mean, after all, you would have spent too long building up those businesses to give them up now right?

Pockface: [angrily] That's not the same thing and you know it!

Me: [defiantly] OK, so, if you would have been cheating people in a shady used car dealership, or had been a con man, or had worked at a casino, or had been a police officer, or been in the military, then the same thing? You'd just keep doing those professions too because you already spent too long doing them? Yet at the same time, you would dissuade your brothers from doing them? (Note to non-JWs: these are all professions that JWs would never do, the reasons why, I don't have the space to explain here.)

Pockface: Those are not...

Me: [cutting him off] The same thing, yeah, I know. No example I could give you would be the "same thing" because you want to justify doing something yourself The Society recommends we shouldn't do. You know, I'm sick of this double standard from you guys who have already feathered your cushy beds, but discourage us young people at the same time from following in your own footsteps. At Bethel, the doctors, lawyers, computer professionals, and such, are treated like gods there; all of these professions require college education. Bethel begs to get people like that there, and then when they do go, they treat them special above the rest of us. Many of them don't even live with us as they get their own housing, cars, food and everything else. They can come and go as they please. They get more money for being there, and so on. Yet, The Society keeps on giving hypocrites like you the same tired line to tell us that we shouldn't go to college because it is worldly, and you regurgitate that drivel, even though you yourself spend every waking work day at a college!

Pockface: Look...

Me: [cutting him off again] No! I'm done trying to talk and reason with you and with people like you!

Some "family friend" he turned out to be. True to my word, I never spoke to Mister Pockface again.

I eventually left Bethel, finished my college education and worked my way up the professional ladder using what I learned to build a real career. Now, it's my turn to be treated special. As I write this, I am looking out of my home office window at the beautiful lake my house sits on, thinking about my wonderful career which gives me generous and ample vacation and personal time off per year. I like my work so much, I can hardly take that time off from it because I really don't need to; at times my job doesn't even feel like work. I work mostly from my own home, that is, when I'm not traveling the world to exciting cities and locations in different U.S. states, and even other countries, staying at nice hotels and resorts and eating great food. I do this travel all on my company's dime, while interacting with intelligent, educated, accomplished, and interesting people.

My career is one in which I wake to up every day looking forward to working in. It is one that has earned me worldwide recognition. It is one that gives me pride, fulfillment, and honor, while allowing me to provide for my family and make enough money to retire comfortably. I am now truly living the dream I always had about how my work life would go.

The main thing I wish to convey here, especially to the younger people who might be reading this, is that I wouldn't have <u>any</u> of it if I had listened to The Society about higher education, or if I had heeded the advice of two-faced, sanctimonious people like Mister Pockface. They would want me to be still making books in their factories for them with zero use of my talents, zero satisfaction in my work, zero money in the bank, and zero to look forward to except praying for Armageddon to come and save me from my tedious existence.

My point here is to tell everybody who will heed my example that regardless of your age, and regardless of how much time The Society has taken from you, there is <u>always</u> time to pursue an education or learn skills that will improve your life. <u>This is simply your right as a human being</u>. You should go for it. And, if you haven't started, then I strongly urge you to start right now.

Look, money isn't everything, but this isn't just about money. It's about making the most of your life and doing what gives you pleasure and meaning in it. It's about doing what you were called to do. It not only doesn't hurt anybody else, it actually improves your world, and everybody else's with whom you come into contact. What is life about anyway? If you believe in God, do you really think He wants us to simply exist, toiling at work we hate every day, just because Armageddon is coming soon? So what if it is coming soon? Should we stop living because of it? Weren't the "prudent virgins" in Jesus' parable praised for being prepared for anything? Why are JWs not prepared for their own future then?

To me, this is also about satisfaction in life and the ongoing confidence that comes from personal success. Sure, chasing money can wreck a person's life or ruin one's soul, but make no mistake about it, simply being poor can do that too. It is pure nonsense to argue that there is some sort of virtue in being broke or of little means. It's also silly to think that doing menial labor your entire life is the way to go, just to avoid talking to people in college who may not agree with your views on things, which is what JWs are so afraid of. If you don't have your own mind, and you're that weak in your own convictions and principles, then you're going to have problems in life no matter which path you take, college or no college.

I think back about the specious Mister Pockface and recall that his wife left him for somebody nicer, younger, and better looking (which was not hard for her to find). He went and replaced her by quickly marrying a vain, ditsy, flaky girl about half his age who had big, floppy, downward pointing boobs she liked to flaunt in tight or low cut blouses.

The congregation was shocked that Elder Pockface wouldn't be more sensible to marry any number of fine, mature, available, older sisters who were in his own age group. They were so surprised by that because, after all, they heard him many times teach from the Kingdom Hall podium about finding a chaste, suitable, spiritually solid marriage mate and about appropriate dating choices for "true Christians."

Given his history of selfishness and double standards, his move didn't surprise <u>me</u> one bit.

False advertisements for a fake future that will never happen

As a young man at God's House, the one place I could get away with saying almost anything was on the factory floor where I worked. Sure, I had my congregation, my tablemates and my roommates, but I pretty much had to be careful about what I said with these people, especially regarding Witness dogma. But, with the brothers I worked with every single day, other young guys just like me with no real authority or importance, well, I could pretty much get away with postulating anything I wanted to.

In this environment, we often had many a discussion about Bible doctrine just to pass the time. Sometimes, the nature of the job allowed more than one of us to be in close proximity of each other for hours on end. So, we had lots of time to discuss nonsense and trivia, hopes and dreams, conjecture and suppositions. When something popped into our heads, we just talked about it. It didn't matter what it was about. Sometimes when we argued or disagreed on something, we would bring it up again later, even if we had already discussed it to death. We did this sometimes just to goad each other into continuing a fight, because it was fun to make each other mad if we could; it was boys being boys. On occasion, teasing or bothering somebody until they were red in the face was hilarious to us, I don't know why. I suppose it was just letting off steam.

One day a discussion about the Earthly resurrection came up. To you non-JWs reading this, please note that Jehovah's Witnesses believe in two classes of people that God will reward: those who will be going to heaven and those who will live forever on Earth. However, either of these rewards may require a resurrection. If you were fated to go to heaven, you would always have to die, but then would be resurrected to heaven. If you were fated to live on Earth forever and you had died, you would be resurrected on Earth. So, that meant there were actually two different kinds of resurrection: the Heavenly and the Earthly. But there was a curious "third" class of people that this story hinges on. These people would also be rewarded to live on Earth forever, but they would be fortunate enough to not need to die at all, ever. They could live right through Armageddon into the paradise Earth and not require a resurrection at all.

Regarding the Earthly resurrection, one Bethelite stated quite confidently that if you died and were resurrected to Earth, you could not be married again, and definitely could not have children ever again either. This was the current understanding at that time by all Jehovah's Witnesses. I forget why it was brought up, but this issue bothered me quite a bit because I had hoped some day to get married and have children. The thought that the simple bad luck of dying before Armageddon arrived and taking with it the hope for me to ever marry, well, that was unthinkable.

However, most Bethelites agreed with this brother, even though many stayed quiet about it and took a neutral position, not arguing it one way or the other. Those who agreed with this brother took their stance based on two things: 1) Luke chapter 20 where Jesus said "those in the resurrection will neither marry nor be given in marriage," and 2) because The Society said so.

I said flat out that they were all wrong.

Unrelenting, I pressed them on this issue by putting an extreme example in front of them about potentially protecting the GB during the "Great Tribulation," a time all Witnesses worried about because we thought that was going to be a time of great testing for all of us. In taking the bait of my example, these folks concluded that if you were to die during the Great Tribulation, even if you died protecting Bethel and the entire Governing Body, you would not be able to marry in the Earthly resurrection. (We always thought that important Jehovah's Witnesses might be especially vulnerable during this critical time, so it might be necessary to put ourselves in harm's way to protect them.) These people said you would not be able to marry even if Armageddon came only a few hours after you died and wiped everything clean for the New Earth. In such a case, when your sorry behind came back in the Earthly resurrection, you could not marry, and you would never be able to have children either.

Too bad. Forget about that family you always wanted.

I thought this was patently unfair, and I was more than a little miffed by this supposition, because they were also implying something else that to me was huge: NO SEX FOREVER! How could it be a Paradise without sex? You see, JWs believe that sex is only for married people. When single, you didn't have it. Well, if you were forced to never be able to marry again, forever, then that meant no sex forever either. When I brought that up, I was told, "Jehovah will take care of that desire for us." I wondered aloud to them if God would zap us with an anti-horny ray or something. They just laughed about that, but gave no real explanation about what that meant.

So, we had a traditional doctrinal back and forth debate on this subject. I brought up the JW arguments like the New Testament really being written for people going to heaven, and Jesus showed this by usually speaking in heavenly terms. Jesus using the phrase "born again" was an example of that, as it obviously meant something spiritual, not literal. I also pointed to the part in Luke chapter 20 where it said, "They can no longer die, but are like angels." Our JW understanding of the Earthly resurrection was that even if we were resurrected to Earth again, it would be possible for us to die at the end of the 1,000 year reign of Jesus, because Satan would be let out to deceive us again. So, if in the Earthly resurrection it is possible that we could die again, then Luke chapter 20 couldn't be talking about that. All of these things told me that Luke chapter 20 pointed to a heavenly resurrection, not an Earthly one.

I even pointed out that if we could not get married, then we would be alone. It was God himself that said in Genesis 2:18, "It is not good for man to be alone." So, this didn't add up to God's original purpose for man, which was to have companionship for life.

I also gave the examples of those in the Bible who we knew were already resurrected on Earth once before, like Lazarus and the little boys and girls who died who were resurrected by the Prophets, the Apostles, and Jesus. The Bible didn't say that they would not be able to marry after their resurrections, did it? It seemed to me that if it were the rule that marriage was not allowed after an Earthly resurrection, the Bible would have mentioned this about these people in particular since they were the first ones to experience it.

My opponents gave me the typical "*Aid Book*" responses at that time, and were not swayed. Nope, they said, if you die before Armageddon, you could not get married in the New System on Earth, nor have children. Period. Case closed.

(I must make a side note here. We had a book at the time called *Aid to Bible Understanding*, nicknamed the *Aid Book*. This book was pretty much the end-all be-all book for Bible doctrine of the JW faith at that time. If you wanted to end an argument among Witnesses about something, this book was considered the case closer. This book was compiled and written in large part by Ray Franz, who happened to be the nephew of Fred Franz, the then current president of the Watch Tower Bible and Tract Society. Ray Franz himself was a Governing Body member just like his uncle was when he finished this book. It's amusing to me now looking back on all those people who stuck by their *Aid Book* responses to refute others in doctrinal arguments, because Jehovah's Witnesses later abandoned this book entirely! You see, Ray Franz eventually left the Jehovah's Witness faith, and then wrote his own book telling his story about why the Jehovah's Witness

Organization and its doctrine was so messed up. JWs aptly felt dubious about that *Aid Book* after that occurrence and no longer used it. Oh well, so much for the *Aid Book* being the last word on JW doctrine.)

Anyway, back to the story, I decided to try a different way to argue against this JW dogma of "no marriage, no children and no sex" for those resurrected on Earth. I am paraphrasing here what I said to these stubborn Bethelites, but it went something like this:

Me: Show me the latest *Watchtower* magazine and *PE* book. [they bring me one each, the latter being a book we named the *Paradise Earth* book which talked specifically about how Earth would look when turned into a paradise.] What pictures do you see here when paradise on Earth is depicted? How are the people shown and how are they comprised?

Them: [discussion result] Well, we see happy smiling people, mostly youthful looking people together and some children.

Me: OK, so mostly people together, that is couples, and their children too? This is The Society's idea of paradise Earth regarding its people there? This is how they show it to everyone who hopes to learn The Truth?

Them: Yes.

Me: OK, so next: How many people will make it through Armageddon alive as couples, together? Give me your best guess or approximation. [please note here that I was under the impression then, like all Witnesses, that only other Witnesses would be saved in Armageddon]

Them: [some discussion] Millions. After all, "Millions now living will never die" is a classic. [please note here that this was the name of a famous sermon given by Brother Rutherford way back in the 1920s in Jehovah's Witness history, which has really since proven to be wrong, but still, JWs cling to this idea.]

Me: Really? Well, first of all, I'm talking couples, not just anybody. Of approximately 3 million Witnesses alive today, you are saying that most of them are couples and most of these couples are married to each other and most of these couples will make it through the worst tribulation in Earth's history intact, together? You want to try that again?

Them: [more discussion] OK then, maybe only hundreds of thousands, a half million couples, a million people maybe, will be on Earth at first, having survived Armageddon and starting the New System of Things.

Me: OK. Fine. Now, how many people will be resurrected to Earth then? Remember, righteous and unrighteous. Discuss.

[Note here: JW's believe righteous people like Noah and Abraham will be resurrected to Earth, but unrighteous people, like those Roman soldiers who killed Jesus and the thief that was crucified with him, will also be resurrected. Why? Because unrighteous people didn't know any better and would be given a chance to learn about God to be saved. Only the "wicked people" would not be given a resurrection, because they knew better and did bad things anyway.]

Them: [after some discussion] Well, there are estimates that we have had eighteen to twenty billion people who have lived so far in history, including the billions now. So, we guess billions in the resurrection, since most of these probably never had a chance to know God. So, maybe fifteen to sixteen billion people coming back or even more.

Me: OK, so you are saying maybe sixteen thousand million, that is, sixteen billion, will be resurrected?

Them: Yes.

Me: Then given those things, why do the *Watchtower, PE* book, and most other Society publications <u>always</u> depict paradise mostly as couples together? With children no less?! Isn't that misleading since most people at that time will be alone, never to be married and never to have children? Billions resurrected alone, and only a few hundred thousand couples at most will be fortunate enough to be married and have children! These few, by the way, only have this privilege because they were fortunate enough to be alive at the right time in history and not die during a horrible "Great Tribulation." So, in paradise, if most living in it will be resurrected and only a fortunate few living in it who were not resurrected being able to marry and have children, then aren't all these pictures in our literature about the New System of things on a paradise Earth <u>false advertisements for a fake future that will never happen</u>?

Them: Whoaaaaa.

Me: To me then, it's as if The Society is promising one thing to hook people in, then teaching an entirely different thing once they got them. That's classic bait and switch if you ask me.

Them: [nervous murmuring, low talking and head shaking]

[silence]

★

I was with a friend of mine later who was also one of the guys in on this factory discussion. We had continued the debate on this subject in private when we both happened to run into George Gangas together. As I mentioned before, I knew this particular Governing Body member pretty well, and I knew that he had a mind of his own, so I took a chance. I brazenly asked him right on the spot what he thought about this subject. I asked him in a way I

174

thought would be provocative, and he responded in a way that was even more so, in a way I'll never forget.

Me: Brother Gangas, in the Earthly resurrection, will Abraham be married to Sarah or not?

Gangas: [getting all dramatic and waving his finger in the air, as he used to be quite a theatrical character] Ahh, well... First, what do you think brother?

Me: I think death severs the marriage union, however upon an Earthly resurrection, we would be free to do again as we please. I think God will allow Abraham to marry Sarah again if he wants to, and if she is agreeable as well.

Gangas: [very dramatically in his Greek accented, old man voice] When Abraham opens his eyes in paradise, he will immediately say, "Where is my beloved Sarah?!" And, upon seeing her he will run to her and hold her in his arms, and hug her and be with her as he always did. After all, he was only asleep! He just woke up! But, Jehovah, upon seeing Abraham approach Sarah, says to him: "No, No, No, Abraham! YOU... SHALL... NOT... TOUCH... HER! FOREVER!"

Gangas: [stopping for even more dramatic effect, then waving his finger in the air] If Jehovah did such a thing... HE WOULD BE A TYRANT!

I couldn't believe what I just heard. Not only did this Governing Body member agree with me that people should be allowed to "be with each other again" after an Earthly resurrection, he stated flat out that it would actually be tyrannical of God to disallow it! This flew in the face of the current JW teaching, and was an example of why I always thought the other GB used to try to keep Brother Gangas under wraps and "use him" much less than the others. He had a mind of his own and would speak it if he wanted to, and this made the other GB nervous.

Still, he was a Governing Body member, and he just agreed with my assertion about this doctrinal issue right in front of my friend. My friend knew I would soon be triumphantly sharing this with everybody else back at the factory the first chance I got.

I thanked Brother Gangas, and then looked over at my friend with my eyebrows raised. He smiled and looked down, shook his head, and said nothing more about it.

Get well soon - We mean it

One day at God's House, I got the flu. We're all human. It happens.

I want to say up front that if you get sick in God's House, the supremely understanding people who run that place realize that this happens. I also want to say, that in the World Headquarters of Jehovah's Witnesses, there is more compassion and patience for the weak human condition than any other place in the world. I further want to say, that at the hub of The Society where the GB rule, when our spiritual brothers are physically ill and are in a time of need and are especially vulnerable, that they are treated better than any worldly place you could ever be in would treat you.

Yes, I really <u>want</u> to say those things, but if I did, I would be lying.

I actually found out that being sick at Bethel was worse than having the sickness itself. Here are some of my reasons why I found being sick at Bethel was a special tribulation:

The Loss of Privacy

First of all, you really don't have any privacy at Bethel to start with, due to the cramped conditions and institutional lifestyle. Now, I don't know about you, but when I'm sick, I don't like to be around other people. I'm not in the best of moods, I feel lousy, I feel ugly, and I am self-conscious about being stinky. I just want to be left alone to sleep.

That is simply not going to happen at Bethel. Unless you are married, you have a roommate who you probably were assigned to, who is basically a stranger to you. He lives with you, sleeps in a bed next to your bed, shares your bathroom, and so on. That is tough enough when things are normal, but it especially sucks when you are sick. On top of that, for about my first year at Bethel, I lived in a four-man room. So, I had to share a room and one bathroom with <u>three other guys</u> I had never met before in my life. Now, try to imagine doing <u>that</u> when you feel your worst.

Then, there are the visits from housekeeping and the nurses. These visits happen on a daily basis, <u>multiple times a day</u>. Try feeling some privacy with all that going on.

The Guilt

Bethel has a mechanism that when you call in sick to your supervisor at work, this puts you on the "sick list." This means you will get numerous visits from a nurse throughout the day, every day, to check your progress. It doesn't matter if you are asleep, she'll knock, let herself in, wake you up and take your temperature, force feed you medicine, give you soup, open your window to let "fresh air" in, and quiz you about how you are feeling. At first, I thought this was nice, until I realized that I could not waive these visits. After a while, I just wanted to be left alone. I knew how to "be sick"; I had been sick before. I knew how to eat soup and I knew how to take aspirin and I knew how sleep on my own without nagging. I didn't need a pain in the ass coming in every few hours to put pressure on me to "get better." To me, this kind of burden was counterproductive to the goal. It just inspired guilt, not healing.

Your overseer may call you. Your table head may call you. Your congregation elders may call you too if you are sick long enough. How many of you reading this have jobs where the employer calls you if you are sick for a few days with the flu? Calling would be OK if you were sick for say, two weeks, or you had an accident and really hurt yourself and was in the hospital. But, this was silly for a simple cold or flu where you might be out for just a few days. In that regard, worldly companies treat their sick employees ten times better than Bethel did.

Finally, you now deal with the guilt of putting out your roommate(s). After all, they want to come home to relax. It's a bummer for them when you are coughing or puking all over the place. You feel really badly about it, but you usually end up running your roommate(s) off. They will only come in to sleep that night and then hurry up to get out of there, to do something else to be away from you. You end up feeling even worse for that reason too.

The Anxiety

After a while, you get hungry for more than soup. But, Bethel only gives you soup when you are sick. If you want more, you have to drag your behind out of bed and get it. I think they do this to "encourage" you to get up. Remember, you are living with thousands of people who share their meals together. Do you really want to have to dress and go down to semi-public place to eat while coughing, sniffling, sneezing or puking? In Bethel, you had to do that at some point if you were sick long enough. Of course, then you'd meet people who would ask you why you were there if you were really sick. They might express concern that you could be getting other people sick by just being there. Or some may imply that if you felt good enough to come down to get food, you certainly could probably go to work soon too, right?

If you were sick for a longer time (say a week or more), you actually could start to feel anxiety that your entire stay at Bethel could be in jeopardy. That is, you would start to get the feeling that you are doing something wrong just by being sick. This was due to the calls from everybody, the visits from everybody and so on. All this starts to add up. I was sick from Monday through Thursday myself. I guess because I got sick on a Monday, that alone was suspicious to them. They hinted that I was just OK that Sunday and went out and had fun, so then why was I sick now on a Monday when the workweek was starting? Hmmm. This seemed dubious to them, like I was being a slacker. They implied that I might be faking it.

Then, after I <u>proved</u> I was sick with the thermometer running 110+ degrees, hacking out a lung, and setting a world record for projectile vomiting, then OK, they'd believe I was really sick. But they then wanted to know <u>how</u> I got sick. Was I doing something silly like exposing myself to outside worldly people? Did I do something foolish like playing in the snow and not wearing a jacket or scarf? What did I do? Tell us, why are you sick?! They'd ask if I got sick often, that is, am I basically a sickly person? If I had pre-existing health problems, why didn't I indicate that in my Bethel application? They bugged me about eating my soup, taking my medicine, brushing my teeth, and gargling often. They asked if I was changing my underwear and sleepers every day. They asked about my bowel movements, and what my stool looked like. They pressed me every day asking when I thought I would get better, and on, and on, and frigging on, the questions came.

The reality of living at this place called "God's House" became even more harsh. I found not only was this no spiritual paradise, it wasn't even a very nice place to be in compared to other worldly jobs and places I had experienced before.

By Friday, I was sick and tired of being sick. After praying about this to give me strength, I drug my behind back into work still feeling a bit lousy. I decided that standing on the cold factory floor still feeling bad, but doing my boring, repetitive, brain-dead work was actually more comforting than being back at my room getting the "Bethel treatment" for being sick.

Today, when I think back about all this, it just makes me sick.

Just beat it

While I was grinding away in a factory at God's House making Bible literature, one of the biggest albums of all time was released: *Thriller*. The individual who released this juggernaut was himself at that time a Jehovah's Witness, which made this event all the more exciting, or aggravating, depending upon your JW perspective. Of course, I'm talking about Michael Jackson, one of the most talented, yet odd people ever to walk our fair planet.

Michael Jackson was not an unknown before *Thriller*, and we JWs certainly knew of most celebrities who claimed to be, or were rumored to be Witnesses. But nothing prepared us, or the rest of the world for that matter, for the immense success and impact of that seminal album *Thriller*. Neither were we prepared for the attention it brought to Jehovah's Witnesses in its wake.

First of all, the songs on this album were played on a then relatively new and unknown TV channel called MTV, short for Music Television. For you young folks out there, this was a time when MTV actually played music videos 24/7. That was its initial claim to fame: All music, all the time. Thus, "Music Television." Secondly, Michael Jackson was probably one of the first black entertainers to show up on this TV channel. Until then, we mostly watched skinny white people sing mostly pop and rock songs in mostly bare bones videos, often in a simple concert setting. Thirdly, MJ proceeded to change the entire genre of music videos, which up until that time were pretty cheesy. Michael made mini-movies for his videos, and they each became an event to watch. Like the rest of the world, Bethelites would gather together to watch whatever music video would be released next from that amazing album *Thriller*, one song after another, each becoming a top ten, and usually a number one hit. Many people to this day believe that Michael Jackson helped make MTV succeed where it was previously struggling.

Anyway, I should mention here that I briefly met Michael Jackson once, and this short meeting had an effect on me. Years before *Thriller,* and before I went to Bethel, I was at a Witness event where he also happened to be. Since he was in fact a Jehovah's Witness at that time, he had to go to meetings, assemblies, and conventions just like all the rest of us. He usually attended with his mother and sometimes his lesser-known sibling Rebbie, who both were to my knowledge the only other Jackson family members who were Witnesses in their adulthood. No other brothers and sisters bothered with that JW stuff, much like their father. If I recall correctly, Michael was touring when the *Off the Wall* album was released, so he attended JW meetings, assemblies and conventions in the cities he visited during his tour.

The circumstance of my meeting him was a bit odd: It was in the men's restroom. I went into the restroom to do my business, and in there was this small, frail, pimply faced black kid with scraggly hair. I really didn't notice him at first, but there he was, small as life, frightened to leave the restroom before the session started because he evidently had been "hassled" while among everyone else. I simply smiled at him and said "Hi" and he said "Hi" back, all the while looking frightened. Because of his countenance, I started to ask him if he was OK, but by then it dawned on me who he was. I had heard earlier of a rumor that he might be at this JW event, but I never imagined I would run into him in this manner. Besides, to me, he didn't look like himself at first glance. By the look on his face, it was tacit that I should not say nor do anything more than just say "Hi" to him. So, I did my business, washed my hands and then smiled at him when leaving, trying to convey with my smile, "Hey, I'm not going to bother you, have a nice day." He just nodded at me, obviously thankful that I left him alone.

Well, that's my "meeting Michael Jackson" story. Big deal, right?

It kind of was a big deal because first, it gave me a perspective on celebrity and how it's not always what it's cracked up to be.

Second, it gave me a sense of compassion for Michael Jackson the person. After I left the bathroom, I of course told other kids that I had just said "Hi" to Michael Jackson in the restroom. The response I got was eye opening. Some people loved the guy, and others hated him, but nobody seemed to be without an opinion. Whenever his name came up, an emotionally charged discussion always ensued.

The fact that Michael Jackson was scared and frightened among his own people, among other Jehovah's Witnesses who should have all loved him en masse like all the other brothers and sisters we allegedly "loved," well, that told me something. Why couldn't this poor guy just be able to come out and mingle with us like anybody else? We were not worldly. As "true Christians," we should not have been unduly impressed with celebrity, so why was Michael frightened by us? Was he just neurotic, this being all his own fault, or could we have contributed to his fear somehow? I didn't understand it that day and couldn't figure it out. I just let it go.

Fast forward to Bethel when I was there, and to the time of *Thriller*. Fast forward to an ever increasingly strange and shape-shifting Michael Jackson, who started out as a young straight black man from Gary Indiana, but who slowly turned himself into an old androgynous white woman from outer space. Michael always gave us something to talk about in Bethel. If it wasn't the Elephant Man's bones, it was the video for the song *Thriller,* that many JWs thought smacked of the occult. But, I must say this, and make this clear: he was still at that time a Jehovah's Witness in good standing.

I should explain to the non-JWs reading this that the "in good standing" means quite a bit in the Witness world. It means that you have not been disfellowshipped nor have you publically denounced the faith. It also means that you have not even been "publicly reproved," which was a sort of probationary period where you could have been DF'd, but were "forgiven" and allowed to stay in the congregation. No, Michael Jackson, with all of his strangeness, was still a JW like all the rest of us. He was still a "brother" to us. He was still worthy of the benefit of the doubt, just as any other brother in the congregation should be. All JWs knew the rules. They knew that unless the elders in his congregation made a move to DF him, or unless Michael Jackson personally announced leaving the JW faith, he was a JW in good standing. Period.

Unfortunately, this was simply not good enough for many young Bethelites. I found this out, much too my chagrin one day, when Michael Jackson himself decided to visit Bethel. He visited us during the pinnacle of the success of the *Thriller* album, which made his visit all the more impacting. Word got around that Michael was in the complex, and the visceral hate of him by many of the Bethel brothers there astounded me. My casual observation of this was that the bulk of the Bethelite brothers who hated him the most were black. This was to me an interesting phenomenon by itself, as I would have thought oppressed blacks should be supporting their similarly oppressed racial brother. But no, they seemed to hate him more than the others did. There were of course white and Latino brothers who joined in the hate as well. They all called Michael Jackson a faggot, or a queer, or a child rapist, or some other similarly nasty thing, often spitting it out with venom.

Now at first, the name-calling was mild, and the teasing was light-hearted. I even joined in on this, saying things like, "Hey, do you think he'll bring Bubbles the chimp with him?" or "I heard he won't stay at any Bethel residence room because we don't have a hyperbaric chamber to sleep in." Ha Ha. Funny stuff. I was guilty of saying things like this myself. We were kids, and Michael Jackson gave us lots to joke about, so can you blame us for that? But after the mild stuff ran out, the name-calling got very ugly. There were of course the gay epithets that were thrown around, as well as the absolute assuredness that he was a child molester. The talk got very, very bad, much worse than how "true Christians" should have been talking, especially at God's House.

After a while, as this discussion deteriorated, a flashback of when I saw him that day in the restroom came to me. I told this story to the guys there in order to try to get them to feel sorry for him rather than hate him. I said that this kind of thinking was probably what made him so uncomfortable to begin with. This didn't work with the haters. Then I started to defend him by saying that there was no proof one way or the other of his sexual orientation, and certainly no proof of the child molesting accusations either. I told them that they were being very un-Christian in their speech about him. I then recited the scriptures about loving each other, and about up building speech.

They responded to that by now attacking me as a "Michael Jackson lover." They started to say that maybe we did more in that restroom together than just say "Hi," and maybe that is why I liked him so much.

Wow. Nice place. What a "spiritual paradise" I was in.

The guy leading this ugliness was by far the most outgoing of all of us in that group. He was one of the oldest, and was the tallest, the loudest, and the most assertive. He was the "big dog" of that floor among us young people who were not overseers in the factory. He also happened to be one of the black guys I noticed who was extremely jealous of Michael Jackson. So, after listening to more of this hate speech, I decided I had enough, especially after they began to turn on me.

I asked that big guy (who I will call Brother Big Dog) if he knew for an absolute fact that Michael Jackson was gay, or that he was a child molester. I confronted him personally on this in front of everybody there, repeating that simple question over and over:

"Do you know this for an absolute fact?" Brother Big Dog tried to make a joke of this by answering with that stupid saying, "Well, if it walks like a duck and quacks like a duck..." He laughed at his own cleverness, and others laughed with him.

But I didn't let that go. I asked him again, did he have proof of his assertions or not? I then added that if he did have such proof, he had an obligation to go to the elders in the congregation and tell of the sin that he knew of. So, I told him that he needed to go right now and tell the elders about this. Now, for the sake of you non-JWs out there reading this, I should make it clear that it is a well understood rule among Jehovah's Witnesses that if you know of sin being practiced by a fellow JW, and do not report it, then you are guilty of sin yourself, participating in and enabling this sin. This was not a good situation to be in, as you could get into lots of trouble yourself just for what somebody else was doing. So, I was in effect using this rule against brother Big Dog.

Of course, Brother Big Dog did not have any such proof. So, after my pushing the issue and not letting him wiggle out of it, he had to say he didn't have any proof that what he was saying about Michael Jackson was a fact. Next, I asked him if Michael Jackson was a brother "in good standing" or not. He also had to answer that yes, as far has he knew, Michael Jackson was a brother in good standing.

I then went up closer to Brother Big Dog, looked him in the eye, and said, "OK then. I myself am witnessing slander by you of a brother in good standing right here, right now. You are doing this in front of all these other brothers as my witnesses. I myself am now obligated to report this. For the record, you are declaring that a fellow brother is gay, and is also a child molester, over and over again with no proof. This is slander, plain and simple." I paused. Brother Big Dog began to look worried because I was not smiling when I said this.

I continued: "Because you are my friend, and because I hope you don't really mean the ugly things you are saying about another brother, I will give you a chance to recant what you have said and leave it at that. Otherwise, I will be forced to go to the elders and report your slanderous behavior, which of course will probably lead to disciplinary action against you."

Brother Big Dog said nothing at first. He just looked at me in disbelief. I said to everybody there while he was thinking this over, "Look, I like laughing and joking as much as the next guy. I didn't mind playful teasing about this Michael Jackson stuff like everybody else. But, this conversation has gotten far too ugly, and is something I have never seen this bad before among us. I think this is embarrassing for all of us. If the older guys among us don't have the sense to stop this kind of talk, then I will do it."

Brother Big Dog told me, "OK man. You're right. We're just playing, OK? You're right, we went too far. We'll stop." He gave me a "bro hug" and told me, "Man, you're all right." He then tried to change the subject to something lighter. The rest of the group got quiet and we all just went on with our work without saying much of anything else for a time.

So, that was the day I defended Michael Jackson on principle in front of all my work mates. I did this even though I had my own doubts about Michael myself. Unfortunately, after that, I had to witness repeatedly more perplexing and more bizarre behavior by this famous "brother." Every time I saw something new that came out in the news about MJ, I would cringe because I had put myself on the line for this guy. I felt more stupid about it as time went on. Of course, the guys at the factory would say things like, "Hey Brock, you hear what your boy did yesterday?" By then I was just beat down by it all, so I just smiled, shook my head, and prayed silently to give me the strength to say nothing more.

Eventually, Michael Jackson declared himself no longer a Jehovah's Witness. This is what JWs call "disassociation," which is pretty much like disfellowshipping oneself. At that point, he was no longer a JW "brother." This was actually a huge relief in the JW community, and was especially so to me.

Still, before that day came, while Michael Jackson was still a JW in good standing and doing one nutty stunt after another, all I could tell myself was that I sure wished he would "just beat it."

You're wrong Brother, so let me join you

As a young man at God's House, I used to have a pretty regular workout routine. I would walk to the gym from The Towers building where I lived and ate my meals, all the way down to the bottom of the hill to 112 Columbia Heights. This is where the weight room was hidden. It was in a dark dank basement, set aside for us young men who wanted to do that kind of activity. As I mentioned before, some GB disliked that we played sports, but others seemed especially bothered that we did something as vain as working out with weights. One GB, Brother Klein, even made fun of us one day saying to the entire Bethel family that those of us that did that were, "Just egotistical because we all just wanted to pump up our bodies to get attention."

Hmmm, well, he did have a point there. But did he need to put it that rudely to try to embarrass us all like that? Was this something that needed to be said by an actual Governing Body member? Really though, is it such a bad thing for a young person to do, working out that is? Wasn't it our own free time and our own bodies that we were dealing with? Did we hurt anyone by working out? Hasn't science proven that a regular workout routine actually improves one's health? What the heck business was it of anybody's if I wanted to work out my own body anyway?

Today, as an older man, I just smile with nostalgia when I see young men talking about working out. I encourage them when I see them getting excited about sculpting their bodies. I tell them that they are looking good, but to make sure they don't overdo it, and especially to stay away from the drugs that are touted as helping with muscle growth, like steroids. Of course, I wish I could do what they are doing now, but I can't take it to that level any more. Even though that is true, I never feel jealousy or feel bothered in the least seeing younger guys get into shape. I've always wondered why petty old men like Brother Klein had such a bee in their bonnet about it. To me, a truly spiritual person should

189

be well above worrying about things like that. I never understood that then, and I still don't to this day.

I realize that I'm going on a tangent here, but it's because Brother Klein angered me so much when he said that about the young men like me who lifted weights. It made me see red for days. Now let me refocus on the main story, which has a similar theme.

That theme was that the life of a Bethelite was about being told what to do for absolutely everything. I grew to resent this considerably during my journey at God's House, and this is in fact one of the key reasons why I eventually left the faith, as I don't believe "true Christians" should be so controlling. True followers of Christ should be patient, warm, loving, generous, kind, easy to live with, and would care about what matters to their brother, not focusing on their own wants. They wouldn't sweat the small stuff because Jesus didn't. After all, Matthew 11:30 said His yoke was to be easy and his load light. The Bethel yoke and load was as strangling and heavy as anything I have ever experienced in my life before or since. If this Bethel life was truly the prelude to the New System of Things as Jehovah's Witnesses claimed, then I would come to realize that I didn't want any part of it. I know it sounds dramatic to say, but if the proposed "Paradise Earth" was to be like this place, that is living with a bunch of ugly, controlling, and judgmental Jehovah's Witnesses forever, well, being asleep in death seemed preferable. At least I'd have peace.

Getting back to my story, it was not that this was such a bad walk to the bottom of the hill to the gym. The walk I took from The Towers building to the factory every day was longer than that. It was just that I usually had to do this walk in the dark because that was the only time I could get to do a workout. So, after dinner I walked to the gym, and after my workout I walked back home in the dark.

This one particular evening I was coming out of the gym to walk home, and an older brother was there right outside the door waiting. It seems that they had recently set up a shuttle because two JW's were mugged in that area earlier that month. In order to get home safely, this older brother was waiting for the shuttle to take him to the living quarters of Bethel many blocks away.

I knew about the shuttle, but to me it was for "old folks." I thought I was invincible in those days, and nothing would happen to me. I was a seasoned Bethelite by that time, walking many times in the middle of the night to do watchman duties and such, so why worry now? After all, The Society didn't care that I walked even further to the factory and back, in the wee hours of the morning to do the assignment they forced me to do. This watchman duty walk was through arguably a more dangerous area than where the gym was anyway. So, why should I be concerned about a shorter walk in more favorable hours of the day from the safer gym location? It seemed like silly reasoning to me that they had this shuttle at all. I mean, they showed they didn't care about us younger folk that much to begin with by making us walk to our watchman duty alone in the dark, so to me the shuttle was set up specifically for these older folks in mind.

Well, this older brother saw me bounce out of the building and start to walk back home. He called after me:

Him: Hey, brother! Where you going?

Me: [walking, not turning around] I'm walking home.

Him: [calling louder to me as I am walking away] **There's a shuttle here for us you know?!**

Me: [still walking, not turning around] OK, thanks. I don't need one.

Him: [running after me] **Hey, let me join you!**

Me: OK. [I stop and wait for him]

Him: [catching up] This is not a good idea. This is dangerous.

Me: [walking together back to the living quarters now] What do you mean?

Him: Well brother, the shuttle was set up for our safety. You really should be using it.

Me: [I play dumb] Our safety?

Him: Yes, there was a mugging around here last week, didn't you hear?

Me: Yeah.

Him: Well, this is really foolish exposing ourselves like this. The Society sets these things up for a reason you know. We really should take advantage of Theocratic arrangements made for our benefit.

Me: Then why'd you come with me?

Him: Uh, well, I figured it would be safer, uh, with us both together.

Me: If I'm not mistaken, it was <u>two</u> brothers together that were mugged, right?

Him: Yes.

Me: Then how does your joining me make this any safer?

[awkward silence]

Him: Well, I guess it doesn't. [pause] Look, let's go back, we're...

Me: [cutting him off] Look, brother, you can come with me if you like, or you can go back and wait for the shuttle, I really don't care either way. But what option you <u>don't</u> have is to nag me all the way home, OK?

Him: [meekly] Sorry.

[We walk in silence for a bit.]

Him: You're probably getting tired of being told what to do by everybody all the time, aren't you?

Me: Very.

We walked along and began to talk, and in our discussion I found out he was a District Overseer, and if I remember correctly, it was of the New York area somewhere for many years before he came to Bethel. I was probably less than one third of his age, and he was a full-time servant longer than I had been alive, yet I had just bitten his head off. This didn't happen every day at Bethel, I can tell you that.

I felt bad about that at the time, but I was physically and emotionally tired, so I didn't feel too bad. He was perceptive though. The thing was that by that time I <u>really</u> was getting sick of everybody, <u>and I mean everybody</u>, trying to tell me what I could and could not do with every stupid little thing. It was exasperating.

For example, one of my roommates barged into the bathroom while I was shaving over the sink one day and turned off the water that was running. He told me I was wasting it, and then proceeded to explain the best way to shave to conserve water. I once woke up with a crick in my neck only to be summarily sent to the chiropractor by my supervisor, even though I didn't want to go. He said it could "get worse" if it wasn't treated and I had to go. I once went outside on a summer day to play a sport of some sort,

193

and then was "counseled" by a guy I didn't even know who told me my shorts were too short. He said I was showing off "too much leg" and that the sisters in Bethel might be offended. (I never had any sister say such a thing to me. This was all in his head.) I was returning from a party one day, going up to my living quarters, and I was wearing a very trendy '80s looking vest with lots of zippers and things hanging off of it. I was told by an old guy in the elevator who just happened to see me that my clothes were worldly.

When all this stuff happened, I just swallowed it. Well, I was done with playing nice by this time. So, now back to the shuttle story, here I had this old guy telling me I was "endangering myself" for not taking the shuttle. This was another classic example of the controlling behavior that I promised myself I would not put up with any more from a random "nobody." This old guy wasn't my friend, he wasn't my roommate, he wasn't my parent, he wasn't my congregation elder, he wasn't my table head, he wasn't one of the many factory overseers I reported to, he wasn't GB, he wasn't my Circuit Overseer, he wasn't my District Overseer, he wasn't the housing elder, he wasn't a policeman, he wasn't the train conductor, he wasn't a judge, he wasn't a bailiff, he wasn't anybody to me!

He was just some old guy who happened to be another JW who had me within eyeshot. Yet this guy still felt compelled to "counsel" me. His prattle didn't even make sense because I don't think he even believed the shuttle was necessary. He was simply trying to convince himself to use it, and at the same time, trying to make himself feel better by projecting blame on me for not taking that shuttle.

I shut this guy down good and made him feel stupid. Frankly, he deserved it.

Even though I felt bad about it at the time, I sure don't today.

No sex? I'll drink to that!

When I was in God's House, it was during the days of the ever-present boom box, and rap was in its infancy. A young Vin Diesel was using his pent-up energy doing break dancing in the streets of New York City on flattened cardboard boxes to the *Double Dutch Bus*. We Bethelites had to have an outlet for our pent-up energy as well. Except there was no way they'd let us "pop and spin" at God's House. We had to think of something else.

Some guys spent their energy lifting ever-increasing amounts of iron. Other guys preferred to play basketball or some other sport. But, by and large, the one outlet that seemed to be shared by most young single Bethel men was drinking. Beer was the most popular choice of alcoholic vehicle used for relaxing away the time. The stories of Bethelites spending most of their hard-earned extra cash on beer, only to drink all of it away each weekend, were so common that they didn't even raise an eyebrow. Others like me who didn't like beer as much, drank harder liquor. I was a Southern Comfort guy in those days, but I would drink anything another Bethelite offered me. Not many people I knew drank wine because it was deemed kind of "girlie." Margarita parties were very common in Bethel, so I'd drink those if they were available. If you were short on cash and still needed "the taste," you could drink Night Train or some other cheap rotgut that was usually reserved for winos.

Yeah, sometimes it got that bad.

I had a friend from Puerto Rico with "connections" who regularly sent him Bacardi 151. Sometimes he would bring it back with him to Bethel after he visited Puerto Rico. Having all those rum based drinks in his room was the best, because those drinks were always guaranteed to be strong, and he seemed to have an endless supply of the stuff. Even though I wasn't a rum guy per se, free booze was the best booze, so I would say, "Bring on the Daiquiris!"

I was always perplexed by the fact that drinking like this was OK at Bethel. Certainly they could have straight out forbidden us to have any alcohol at all. However, JWs believe that alcohol in moderation is OK as the Bible is full of examples of that, Jesus being a primary example of a wine drinker. Still, that didn't mean that Bethel couldn't forbid it. After all, Jesus never drank Jim Beam, or chugged a six pack of Corona. They forbade mustaches on white guys and beards on all men in general, didn't they? They forbade R-rated movies too. So why not forbid all booze except wine? Heck, why not forbid wine too? Show me in the Bible a place that said you shouldn't wear a beard or mustache. Show me where it said you couldn't watch an R-rated movie. To me, the Bible itself was at least R-rated. Life is R-rated. Still, if you were known to watch these kinds of movies at Bethel, you could get kicked out for it. Yet, I could show you at least a dozen places in the Bible that told of the folly of too much drink, and others that flat out condemned over drinking and drunkenness. This was a very clear issue of sin the Bible didn't equivocate on. That said, over drinking was common at Bethel anyway! This to me was another example of the way Jehovah's Witnesses enforced "selective sin," making some sins worse than others, in ways the Bible didn't really support.

Since they didn't forbid beer, wine and other liquor at Bethel, the young guys took full advantage of that. I won't claim that most of them got drunk, because they didn't. I never got drunk myself at Bethel either. But, I will say that some Bethelites did get drunk, and when they did, it was well known who it was and when it happened. Also, many at least "drank too much" until they were silly or sloppy, buzzed if you will. Still, these things were all overlooked at Bethel as long as you did it in the privacy of your own room, and didn't cause a stir in any other way. I found out many years later for example that Brother Hanger Man was himself a drunk. That's probably why he smelled funny and mumbled so much. But, he was old and had been at Bethel his entire life, knowing many of the original JW founders, and knowing a whole lot about The Society's skeletons. As long as Brother Hanger Man didn't make this drinking habit public, and he kept those skeletons in the closet, the Bethel powers that be just let him be. They gave him a nonsense job to do that also allowed him enough spending money to drink himself to sleep every night.

The strangeness of allowing this kind of behavior was juxtaposed with the very strict rule of not allowing R-rated movies (as I mentioned before). Consider this: they were extra rabid and extra hard on anybody who would dare bring a girlie magazine into Bethel. If you did this even one time, you were out. The "no pornography" rule at Bethel was put into place because of an interesting chain of thinking that the Governing Body used: If you looked at pornography, then you were obviously masturbating. Masturbation in turn led to homosexuality. Many thought that homosexuality was a worse sin than heterosexual immorality because it is "against nature."

So the Bethel equation on this issue was simple: Pornography = Masturbation = Homosexual perversion.

OK, let me explain this for those of you who are not JWs, because this chain of thinking might all sound a bit strange to you.

First, the point of pornography leading to masturbation should not be a stretch to accept. That's what pornography is mostly used for. Nobody in their right mind will claim otherwise. Sure, there are guys that are so hardened to general nudity that they actually might read *Playboy* magazine for the articles, but still, even those guys could find the type of porno that would work for them as a masturbatory vehicle. So, the "Pornography = Masturbation" part of the equation I don't have a problem with. It's generally true.

The other thinking the GB had about this was that the words of Jesus should be heeded in Matthew 5:28, "But I tell you that anyone who looks at a woman lustfully has already committed adultery with her in his heart." Hence, the thought was that if you looked at pornography, then you were committing this sin. Now, I don't have a problem with that point either. Keep in mind though, if Jesus' words were taken literally, my guess is most JW men would be DF'd, and most married JW men would end up being divorced as adulterers. Jesus simply <u>had</u> to be speaking in hyperbole, not literally. His statement about "adultery in his heart" is not much different from when he used the "camel through the eye of a needle" statement. It was purposeful exaggeration to make a point.

That said, I would like to add some reality into this discussion. If a guy is not exposed to pornography or the naked human female body for a long enough time, he will then be in a state most of us Bethelites were in: turned on by anything that was even remotely sexual. When a man is young and has raging hormones, absolutely anything can be a cause for a masturbatory thought. If, for example, we were to see a woman bend over for some reason from the front, well, her cleavage might give us an instant erection. If we were to see her from behind, the same result. If we were to happen upon a *Sports Illustrated* swimsuit edition or a *Victoria's Secret* catalog, we might be struggling with those images while trying to go to sleep that night.

Guys reading this, you know what I mean. Don't pretend you don't. Girls reading this, please understand that's the way men are built, it's not our fault. Maybe it's our father Adam's fault, I don't know. Please, work with us here. The only guy who doesn't have this problem from time to time is a eunuch, and you ladies don't want that guy. I once heard a joke about this issue that went this way: "They did a study of a thousand males between the ages of eighteen and sixty. They found that 9 out of 10 of these men admit to masturbating at least occasionally. They also found 1 out of 10 of them lie."

The next part of the equation, the "Masturbation = Homosexuality" thing, that's where it starts to get strange. For some reason, maybe because it occasionally happened at Bethel, I don't know, The Society was convinced that if you masturbated enough, you would eventually do it in front of other guys! That in turn would lead you to start masturbating the other guy, and he doing the same for you. After that, it was off to the homo races doing everything else. Look, I struggled with this "self abuse" issue while at Bethel just like every other red-blooded American guy there. This was a subject of many of my prayers to God actually. But there was no way in hell I was ever letting another dude see me naked that way, let alone allow another guy to touch me. I don't care how horny I got.

But that's just me, I guess.

Now, I never did get where The Society came up with why they were so convinced masturbation lead to gay behavior. The only thing I could think of is that since living in the institution that Bethel is, with all its restrictions, and it being the closest thing in the JW world to a Catholic Priest's rectory, maybe The Society knew something I didn't. Maybe when you deprive people of something normal and natural like sex for long enough, and then pile them up on top of each other close enough, they will in fact begin to hump each other. Still, if that were true, that didn't mean that the "Masturbation = Homosexuality" thing had any merit in general; it might only have merit when coupled with the unnatural living conditions in places like Bethel.

Or prison.

(Side note: While I was there, I never knew of anybody who was homosexual, nor was I ever propositioned there. The idea of gays at Bethel seemed a bit foreign to me. However, there were many stories that flew around about this subject, none least of which was one such story of sixty or so Bethelites all getting kicked out of Bethel for homosexuality at the same time in the late 1960s. There were also stories of a few Bethel "heavies" who were gay, most notably Brother G-, who was a GB at one time who many whispered was gay when I was there. I didn't believe it at the time though. It turned out later to be a proven fact, but only after the rest of the GB tried to quietly get rid of him after he molested a young boy. Even though pedophilia and homosexuality are not necessarily related to each other, after Brother G- was ousted, the fact that he had homosexual relationships with other Bethelites also came out. Plus, the pedophile stuff about him also came out, and both issues became proven fact. Sheesh.)

You should note though, that in Bethel, other people did all of your laundry, which included washing your underwear and changing your bed sheets. It would be easy for them to know if you were whacking off, since, how could you hide it? That alone was a sobering issue for most of us and actually, in a perverse way, this helped me to avoid it. However, there was always the occasional "nocturnal emission." Many of you ladies out there might not know this, but if a man doesn't ejaculate in one way or another after a long enough time period, his body will take care of this build up for him subconsciously in his sleep. What happens is we might just be having a great dream one night, and then wake up with soiled sheets, completely innocent of anything more than that. It is often referred to as a "wet dream." Yes folks, that meant that even Jesus Christ himself must have experienced this, just like every other natural human function, because he was in fact an adult human male.

Well, obviously the Bethel powers that be knew of this physical phenomenon that almost all adult males experience, especially young males who are deprived of sex, and instructed to refrain from masturbation. The occasional nocturnal emission would of course have to be overlooked. Still, you better not have this happen too often, because it could only mean that you were doing this on purpose. That would not be tolerated.

Regarding the issue of homosexuality, I've never been sure why, but to most JWs this was way worse than heterosexual fornication. They all thought, "Homos were like those Sodomites of old who had fire and brimstone rightfully hailed upon them. Heck, society even named a sex practice after those perverts."

Personally, I never struggled with gay thoughts myself, and I did find the sodomy practice a bit disgusting, even for heterosexuals. From a strictly moral viewpoint, however, I didn't see why homosexuality was worse than other sins. After all, the Bible didn't say that fairies would be tossed into the Lake of Fire first, before red-blooded American "normal" fornicators did it? That said, I gave gay people a break because I figured that human sexuality was complex. Who knows why people do what they do? I mean, everybody has their weakness. It's easy to condemn people with weaknesses that aren't ours.

I would often make this argument with JWs on this subject by bringing up hermaphrodites, that is, those people born with both sets of genitals. "What about them?" I would ask, with no good answer ever given me. Some of these had their parents and doctors surgically alter their genitals to make them normal. Basically, their sex was chosen for them by somebody else. Could you really blame these poor people if they grew up confused about their sexuality? I couldn't. I also wondered, could it be possible for this mix-up or confusion to happen to people on the inside, in the brain where the sex drive really comes from, without the obvious physical outside issues of a hermaphrodite? I wasn't sure then and I'm still not sure now.

So, to wrap up my observations about the two issues of sex and booze at Bethel: I saw young guys in their early years allowed to blow off steam by drinking themselves silly every weekend, something specifically condemned in the Bible. They did this to get relief from the intense pressure caused by the day-to-day grind of the Bethel schedule. But those same guys would in turn be required to wait and pray for the occasional wet dream, in order to get relief from the other, much more intense pressure of no sex whatsoever.

I guess I'll drink to that.

The Bethelite Things

(Sung to the tune of *My Favorite Things* from the musical *The Sound of Music*)

Backward masked music that gets you ejected

Overtime working that makes you dejected

Stern overseers who all act like kings

These are a few of The Bethelite Things

Sisters who visit in bright colored busses

Coming to see you is one of the plusses

Until you find out they want wedding rings

These are some more of The Bethelite Things

When your insights

Are shunned outright

It might make you mad

So you should remember that you matter not

And then you won't feel

Too bad

Noisy housekeepers and stern ugly nurses

Empty men's wallets and barren girl's purses

Gulping your food down before the bell rings

These are just some of The Bethelite Things

Long boring worship that goes on for ages

Toiling long hours for less than no wages

Just one mistake and you suffer some dings

These are a few of the The Bethelite Things

When the food bites

And the drink stinks

It makes me feel real sad

I simply remember that I'm leaving soon

And then I don't feel

So bad

Lady and the Chump

Well, one day it finally happened. My journey to God's House was thrown off track when I met a girl. I had in fact met dozens of girls, heck, maybe hundreds in the years I was there. Though none of them were like Charity. I'll call her Charity because the name fits her, and her real name was something close to that.

Charity visited Bethel during a Fourth of July one year. While we didn't openly celebrate this holiday with the worldly people, we were allowed to go outside to enjoy the fireworks like everybody else. New York City always gave a great fireworks display, and we could watch it on the roofs of our various Bethel residence buildings. We would see the fireworks explode over the harbor near the Statue of Liberty. Charity came with her parents, younger sister, and brother. She knew some of the Bethelites I knew. Since she was from New Jersey, she actually had visited Bethel quite often by the time we met. Since meeting Bethelites wasn't something all that unusual for her, she didn't act like many of the first time visitor girls who came from far away. She had a maturity and a calm coolness about her that stood out.

She also had beauty that stood out. Her features were all very traditionally feminine, her nose tiny and perky, her teeth and smile perfect, her eyes piercingly beautiful, her hair long and flowing past her shoulders. She had a sly little smile, a gentle laugh, and a wonderful slender figure with ample enough curves in the right places to suit my tastes. To me, she had a sort of princess aura about her, definitely a lady. Beauty evidently ran in her family, as her mom was quite attractive, and her little sister, who was much more outgoing than Charity, was doing some modeling.

I first laid eyes on Charity at a very crowded gathering at Bethel that Fourth of July evening. This gathering had many Bethelites coming and going from it, and I caught her eye when she was surrounded by about a half dozen guys. She glanced over and smiled at me, but that's all she did. I noticed that she graciously chatted with every Bethelite who approached her, and she seemed genuinely interested in what they had to say. I kept glancing over and moving myself into her line of sight to see if I could get the nerve up to introduce myself. I caught her eye more than once, looking for an opening. Luckily, a Bethelite I knew personally started talking to her when some others moved on, so I took that as my cue to make my move. I went up to her at that point, and then after acknowledging my friend, I said:

Me: Hi. I'm Brock.

Charity: Hi. I'm Charity.

Me: Nice to meet you Charity. You seem to know many people here. Do you visit Bethel often?

Charity: Yes, actually, we do. My parents know lots of Bethelites. [motions over to where they are] We're from [nearby New Jersey town] so we come here quite a bit. We love to visit Bethel. [big smile]

Awkward silence ensues as I lose myself in her beauty. I neglect to say anything clever, or much of anything at all. Good-looking women didn't intimidate me in general, but this girl had me speechless. My friend, who already knew her, breaks the silence and talks a little bit to us both. He then excuses himself. I remember being a little irked at him for never mentioning this lovely creature to me before.

Charity: [breaking the silence] Uh... so, are you from Hawaii? [playfully smiling while obviously looking at my shirt]

Me: What? Oh! [looking down at myself I realize I have on a very loud Hawaiian shirt] No, no, I'm not from Hawaii. [chuckling] I guess I just like this shirt. You'll have to speak up a bit though, I can't hear you over this silly thing!

Charity: [laughs]

Me: Do you like Hawaii?

Charity: Well, I've never been. I do think I would love Hawaii if I ever got to go there, and I do want to go someday. I think it would be so beautiful. I would love to just play on the beaches there... Wouldn't you?

Me: Sure... um... wait – I remember now. I actually <u>am</u> from Hawaii! If you watch the fireworks with me on the roof later, I'll tell you all about it!

Charity: [Laughing] OK. We'll see... [giving me a sly smile, knowing quite well that I was full of it]

Well, Charity and I kept on talking. We didn't go on the roof at that point, but we didn't stop talking either. I just couldn't help myself as I shamelessly teased and flirted with this lovely lady right from the get go, full out. I don't know what got into me. I guess you can only chalk it up to chemistry... or hormones. Other guys butted into our conversation, but I didn't leave her just because another Bethelite started talking to her. This wasn't all that unusual anyway in a place where the available men out numbered the available women by a far margin. Of course, I didn't blame them for butting in; she was awesome. We were all just trying to find out what we could about this pretty little lady in our midst. It seemed that everybody wanted to meet her.

At one point, when yet another dude was introducing himself to her, I interrupted and told her that I should probably go. You see, I figured by then I had made some time with her, and it went well. If I stayed around any longer, well, I would become a pest. I told her that it was really nice meeting her and that I hoped we could speak again before she left. As I turned to go, she lightly touched my forearm and told me to hold on. She then finished up the conversation with the other brother. She turned and focused on me, and told me with a smile that she wanted to go on the roof to watch the fireworks with me after all.

Wow. I was so stoked.

Since the fireworks were starting soon, she quickly introduced me to her family and told them that we were going to watch the fireworks together. As we left the room, other Bethelites tried to join us, but I gave them the stink eye, shaking my head at them. They got the message and went ahead of us. We went up and watched together, and we stood very close to each other. A crowd gathered behind us to watch too. I tentatively moved her in front of me, so she could get a better view, and stood behind her close enough to smell her hair. It was like smelling an angel. The crowd pressed on us and kind of pressed us together. She didn't mind, and neither did I. I had to put my hand on her waist during this time to keep us steady, sort of like if we were dancing. After a while, I got brave and held her hand. She let me. I couldn't tell which was louder, the fireworks going off over the harbor, or the ones going off inside me.

After the fireworks were over, we went down and found her folks again. We talked some more, and before Charity left, I made sure to get her address and phone number. I promised to visit her the first chance I got. She smiled at me and told me that would be nice, and then she said proper goodbyes to everyone. Always the lady, she simply glanced at me as she left with that sly smile that just killed me dead.

I so wanted this woman.

I wrote Charity right away; I think that next day actually. I told her more things about me and my family, who lived far from her hometown in New Jersey. She wrote me back and told me all about herself and her family. Even though it took more than a month, I was finally able to visit her. I found that her family was down to earth and fun to be with. Over the ensuing months, I wrote her quite a bit, and I visited her too. I'd stay the night in the spare room if I could, taking a friend with me. You see, it was difficult dating in Bethel as we didn't have that much time off, and we were always broke. We couldn't really just go places without lots of planning and saving up.

I tried to visit Charity when I could. I didn't mind if people thought we were dating either, although we probably weren't really. Looking back on it, we only saw each other in groups, usually with her family around. To me, we were dating. I didn't get her alone like I did that first night. I dreamed about kissing her, about touching her, about holding her and about just being with her. I liked other girls while I was at Bethel, but with her I had particularly strong feelings. I had not dated officially during my time at Bethel, because dating was such a serious thing there. For Charity, I would have made an announcement in front of the entire Bethel family that we were dating if need be.

One thing stood in the way of my pursuing her the way I should have. There was one thing that nagged at me from the very beginning. You see, right about the time I met Charity, I had grown to dislike New York City, its weather, its smell, and its noises too. I did like New Jersey because I had lots of pleasant memories from there. Still, to me, New York and New Jersey were both intertwined. Besides, neither of them was my hometown. Also, I began to dislike Bethel itself. As a result, I was in the process of deciding that I had enough of Bethel. It would be some months until I had a Bethel anniversary (the date I originally came to Bethel), and I was telling myself that at that anniversary date, I probably would leave Bethel to return home.

Meeting Charity was in fact one of the few things that made me want to stay. Up until meeting her, all indicators to me were that I would leave Bethel and fairly soon.

But then there was Charity. Was I destined to be with her and never go home again? Would I move to New Jersey to pursue her, or would I stay at Bethel and try to pursue her that way? What if this was simply another case of puppy love I had felt before? How could I attend the college back home that I had been making plans for? How could I afford the ticket to go back and forth between my hometown and New Jersey to pursue Charity, due to the fact that it was a plane ride each way and I was broke? My mind reeled.

I prayed about this quite a bit, but I never told anybody else about this dilemma because at that time I hadn't told anyone that I was thinking about leaving Bethel. Leaving Bethel was just too serious a thing to mention casually. I wanted so much to just pour my heart out to Charity to tell her what was going on in my mind. I wanted to return home, but I also wanted to be with her. What the heck should I do?

On the very next trip to see her, I decided to tell her what I had not told another human being, that is, that I wanted to leave Bethel. I figured that her reaction to this would be very important in my decision about what to do next. I wasn't one hundred percent sure how she felt about me anyway, since we had never gotten physical at all. (This is what good Witnesses do while dating, at least at first.) I figured that maybe I was being silly about it all. Maybe she wouldn't really care all that much if I left Bethel, or even moved away. Perhaps I was just a fun diversion for her, as I knew so many other guys were interested in her too. Maybe I was making this bigger in my mind than it needed to be.

When we were at her house together the next time, I asked her if we could be alone that evening. I had never asked to be alone with her before. She gave me a big smile and said she would like that. Always the lady, I think she wanted to be alone with me too, but she would not make the first move. I really wanted to be alone with her to tell her all of the things on my mind. However, she took it as meaning we should park somewhere and kiss for the first time. It's funny, but that was actually not on my mind that day, because I figured that if we were not going to be together, I didn't want to hurt her feelings by just making out with her and then leaving town. She deserved a gentleman, and I was going to be one.

Later that day, we finally were able to be alone. She drove her car and parked it in a lonely spot. The moon shone on her through the window. She was a vision in a snug little sweater top with her long flowing hair falling over her shoulders and onto her breasts, with her lovely eyes just piercing me. She turned to me, smiled sweetly, moved closer, and looked up at me with adoration. I knew what she wanted: our first kiss. My heart hurt at what I was going to bring up. I hoped it would turn out OK, as I really didn't know exactly what I would say, or how I would say it. I had to bring it up though, now or never.

She stopped smiling at me when I told her I had a very serious issue to talk to her about. I then let it all out. I told her about my wanting to leave Bethel. She was very surprised. She thought I liked being at Bethel. I told her, no, actually, not any more. I spent some time trying to explain why. She was puzzled because she and her family loved Bethel; they were dyed-in-the-wool Witnesses, through and through. What I was telling her made no sense to her because Bethel was something she grew up admiring. She frowned. She asked what I was going to do then. I told her I wanted to go to college, as this was my first priority. She was puzzled about that too and frowned some more. She told me she didn't believe in college for Christians, and neither did her parents. It was strange to her that she only found out now that I was going to pursue college. She also found out that I was giving up full-time service because I was giving up Bethel and I was not going back to pioneering either. I could see the confusion on her face.

This was not going well.

She then asked, "What about us?" I told her she was one of the best things about my stay in Bethel and that I had asked myself that same thing over and over again. I told her that I thought about her every day, and that she had become very important to me. But, I just didn't see myself staying at Bethel. It seemed that I couldn't finish college in New Jersey either. Also, I couldn't stay away from my family at this point in my life. Besides, her family would not support my going to college. I told her I missed home, and that the only reason I held on these last few months at all was mainly because of her. I was using this time to try to figure out what to do about her and that was why I needed to have this discussion with her now.

She was looking a bit annoyed by this time, maybe even a little upset. At this point, however, I had to go on. I then worried to her out loud that long distance romances rarely work out. Even when they do succeed, they have logistics problems forever, with both families spread out, where somebody would have to be away from their own family.

She agreed with me on that last sentiment, but didn't say a whole lot after that. She just sat there looking stunned, and we both sat in silence for a time. As difficult as it was, I came to realize at that moment of silence that we wouldn't be able to go any further with our relationship because I was moving in the opposite direction from her in what she wanted and needed in a man. I also knew I had to be a man. I had to make the hard decision.

I broke the silence by telling her that my anniversary of coming to Bethel was coming up. I had said to myself many months ago that this date would probably be my last day before I returned home. I told her that not seeing each other anymore was what I thought would be best for us both, before we got any more serious, and before this got any more difficult for either of us. I told her I was very sorry.

She moved away from me, covered her eyes with her hands, and started to weep. I was dying inside. I tried to hold back my own tears, but I couldn't. We both just sat there and cried for a short while. She gathered herself up and started the car. I felt like a chump as we drove back to her folk's home in silence. The rest of that evening is a fog for me, even until today, as my heart was truly broken over what I had just done. All I know, is I went back to Bethel and couldn't wait to get back to my hometown now. I just wanted to get this whole damn mess behind me. I wanted so bad to get the hell away from Bethel, New York, New Jersey, the whole blasted rest of it.

A number of weeks later, I got on a jet plane and didn't look back.

About a year went by. I was home now and I had just finished my latest semester of college, I started thinking about Charity again. I guess it was because I had a new girlfriend by that time who reminded me a little of her. Even though my life was going great by then, I still thought about Charity, and what might have been. I decided to write to her, to apologize again for being such a chump in having to leave like I did. I wrote her about how wonderful she was, and how she deserved the world, and that I hoped she was happy, and so on. I remember my hand shaking as I dropped the letter into the mailbox.

I envisioned that she would write me back and ease my conscience. I was hoping that she would tell me that it was OK, that I did the right thing, that she was doing great, and that everything was just fine with her now. I eagerly waited for a response from her, one week then two weeks, one month then two months.

It never came.

I see loser quitter dead people

Well, this was it. It was the mid 1980s and Prince was singing about crying doves, which reminded me of myself. Van Halen was also yelling at us to "*Jump*," which I finally decided to do. I was going to take the jump and end my journey at God's House. Nothing would change my mind about that now because I simply didn't find God there.

The Bethel acceptance letter I got years before stated the minimum time those who went to Bethel were expected to stay for. Well, I kept my word. Actually, I had doubled that time. I thought that was pretty darn good, given that the last several weeks or so of my stay at Bethel was fairly miserable. For some masochistic reason, I had a particular date in mind to make my stay end on an even year. I wanted to leave on the anniversary of my arrival, and on my own terms. I had fought many issues, resisted many temptations, and avoided a maze of opportunities to screw up. I had suffered heartbreak in many ways while there too (like my dilemma with Charity.) With all that, I managed to not get kicked out of Bethel. I even flourished there in some respects. Because of that, I could hold up my head high. I did it!

With a few weeks left to go, I finally gave notice of my leaving to everybody. Now, if you stayed at Bethel for any length of time, you ended up knowing about a zillion people both in Bethel, and locally in the various congregations you attended or visited. It took time to say all the goodbyes, as well as to explain to each and every one of those zillion individuals why you were leaving.

It turns out this wasn't so easy.

As many of you who are Witnesses may already know, if you have ever stopped doing any form of service in "God's Organization," it was not usually looked upon favorably. For example, if you ever stopped pioneering or stopped being an elder or even stopped running microphones in the Kingdom Hall, <u>if you ever stopped doing something you volunteered to do in the first place</u>, then you were a loser. Yep, you were a big fat loser quitter who didn't appreciate "spiritual things." You were now considered a spiritual zero.

The Witness formula is this: "You" + "Stopping volunteer service" = "Loser-Quitter"

After you stopped your service, even if you stayed in the congregation and gave it your all in every other way, you were still the subject of whispers about your shameful trip to Loserville. Well, let me tell you, if you think stopping being an elder or stopping pioneering is bad, then leaving Bethel service makes you a double whammy, double dog loser. You become a loser quitter of epic proportions, to be pitied and shunned.

I found over time that there were only a few good reasons to leave Bethel to avoid this loser stigma. I watched this occur over and over again through the years. This is what I observed:

1. If somebody in your family died, like your dad, it was OK to leave Bethel to help your mom out. They would say: "Go with our blessings brother. Be strong. We love you!" [group hug]

2. If you got deathly ill, that is you got cancer or lost a leg to diabetes or your eyeballs fell out, then it was OK to leave Bethel for that too. They would offer: "Go with our blessings brother. Be strong. We love you!" [bigger group hug]

3. If you were married and your wife got pregnant, well, children aren't allowed in Bethel. They would utter: "Go with our blessings brother and sister. Be strong. We all love you!" [biggest group hug]

If you wanted to leave Bethel for any other reason, then you were spiritually weak, and not worthy of so much as a real goodbye.

Many Bethelites knew this, and contrived stories in order to force themselves into one of the "It's-OK-to-leave-Bethel" categories. For example, some made up a relative dying. Some had a relative who died, but in actuality it was only a distant uncle twice removed whom they never even met. Some got "sick" in a mysterious way with maladies no human doctor could detect. After they got home, they were magically healed. Some "got pregnant" and then after getting home they had an opportunely timed false alarm, so no baby.

You get the idea. They had the "good excuses."

Well, I refused to play that game. I was leaving because I wanted to. I was simply done with Bethel service. I had nothing to be ashamed of and no reason to lie. I had doubled the time The Society expected me to stay, and did it with dignity and hard work. I wanted to go home, go to college, get married, have kids, and just be a normal human being without having to spend the rest of my life living in an institution.

That seems honest and straightforward, doesn't it? After all, Jehovah's Witnesses often talk about "being honest hearted" and "speaking the truth." Certainly, the people I had befriended at Bethel didn't need to hear a variation of the same old excuses everybody else gave to leave Bethel, right? Certainly, my friends could accept honesty from me and wouldn't judge me for being truthful about my reasons for leaving Bethel... they were better than that, right?

To answer that, let me tell you about a conversation I had with a young couple I had grown close to and very fond of in my stay there. They were nice, smart, and attractive people. They had a good sense of humor, and I really liked them. I thought they liked me too. We spent off time hours together laughing and joking, playing in good clean fellowship. I wanted to talk to them more in order to tell them all my hopes and dreams for the future.

Here is how the conversation went with them one day near the end of my stay, as I ate an evening meal with them. With these meals, we could sit anywhere we wanted to sit, and have more time to talk than the other more formal meals. I thought it would be the perfect time for me to talk to them about my future.

We sat and began to eat. I told them I was leaving Bethel. The conversation went something like this:

Him: Oh boy, oh boy. [shaking his head back and forth]

Her: Oh, no... [clasping her hands together]

Him: Yes, we thought we heard that you were leaving, but we didn't believe it. [looking sad, still shaking his head]

Her: Poor thing, we're so sorry.

[this went on for a while...]

Me: Uhh. Guys, sorry? Why?

Him: Well, you're leaving Bethel. Why would you leave here for no reason?

Me: I do have a reason. I'm tired and I want to go home. I did my time. Actually, doubled it.

Her: That time is just to let brothers know they cannot come for a few months and leave. That way they know this is a serious commitment. But it isn't meant to mean that when that time has passed they should leave. [clasping hands even harder]

Him: We're all tired brother. This world tires us all out. Now is not the time to give up. Now is the time to persevere diligently in our sacred work.

Me: Look guys, be happy for me. I've completed my stay here and I did everything I wanted to do. Now, I'd like to go home and lead a normal life.

Him: Normal? What's normal? This is the closest you'll be to living in The New System and you want to return to the outside and work in the world? [still shaking his head]

Her: There is nothing normal about this wicked world brother. We need to keep close to Jehovah's Organization and this is where we can best do that. [clasping hands together so hard, that if you put a pencil between them, the lead would turn into a diamond]

[more hand wringing and expressions of dismay ensue...]

Me: Guys, guys, listen. It's OK, all right? I'm only leaving Bethel, I'm not dying.

Him: [with disgust, spitting it out] It's the same thing.

Me: [urk]

Wow. Now that hurt.

We all stopped talking. I tried to finish my meal, but it was difficult for me to do that as my throat was so tight I couldn't swallow. By then my stomach was in knots too.

I gave up on the meal, and got up and said a weak "good bye" to them. They, not even looking at me in the eye, did likewise. I never saw nor communicated with these two "good friends" ever again.

Do you know what the worst part was? I found out that this wouldn't even be all that unusual. In fact, after years in Bethel service making many friends there and sharing everything with these people, living closely with them, eating every day with them, toiling hard side by side, fending off angry people in field service with them, meeting their families and worrying about their problems and their health and so on, yet upon returning home <u>I would not be able to keep one single friend from that place</u>.

Not a single one.

My sin?

I just wanted to go home.

Epilogue

When I returned home from God's House, I was more lost and in need than when I went in. I returned shell shocked, somewhat like a war veteran. I found out later that this condition was not the least bit unusual for ex-Bethelites. Many left home as heroes, but came back as zeroes. Their journey to find where God lives was over, and they had nothing with which to replace it.

For years, I held many of these experiences inside, telling few people about them. I figured that the fault must have been mine. This is not unlike abused women or children who blame themselves for the things the abuser does to them. When you love and trust someone and then they hurt you, well, you justify it by taking on at least part of the blame.

The alternative was to admit that many aspects of the religion of my youth was wrong, and that I had appeared to waste my time trying to please those who couldn't be satisfied with any amount of sacrifice I made. I just couldn't face that, even in the light of everything I experienced and knew in my gut to be true. Deep down inside, I knew I was not worshipping to please men. My worship was intended to please God. Still, the men and women on Earth were the only physical anchor I had to gauge the success and value of my worship. As a child, how could I begin to gauge it otherwise? Every child needs approval from his parents for the same reason, it's just natural because with youth goes insecurity. We all need approval from men, even as adults, and even if we are in the end worshipping God. When you don't get that approval, you begin to reason, "what's the use of even trying to be good?"

It took me many more years to finally decide that I just could not bear being a Jehovah's Witness any longer, as direct quotes from Jesus Christ rang in my head over and over:

- "Do not judge or you too will be judged by the same judgment. For in the same way you judge others, you will be judged, and with the measure you use, it will be measured to you." (Matthew 7:1,2)

- "By this all men will know that you are my disciples, if you love one another." (John 13:35)

Also, the words of the Apostle Paul rang in my ears as well:

- "If I have the gift of prophecy, and understand all mysteries and knowledge, and if I have a faith that can move mountains, but do not have love, I am nothing." (1 Corinthians 13:2)

After decades of being one, I had to face the fact that Jehovah's Witnesses are all about the judgment of others, and even each other. Their constant sizing up of each other's "spiritual strengths" and "spiritual weaknesses" is simply reprehensible. Their disdain of everyone else who is not a Witness, disgusting. Their works-based religion is impossible to fulfill without self-reproach and trepidation.

Neither do they really love. Not others. Not even each other. Their so-called love is based on merit only. If you do what they like, they'll put up with you. If not, they'll drop you without hesitation and not feel a thing about it. I'm sorry to say it, but this kind of behavior is simply not love.

When I was a Witness, I was just like them too. But, I couldn't see that what I was doing was wrong. As a rule, Jehovah's Witnesses simply can't see this about themselves in the same way people with bad body odor usually can't smell themselves.

By the time I finally broke free of their mentality, I was nearing middle age. I then experienced for the first time in my life what it felt like to really like people, and then to even love some of them individually. It was without the judgmental attitude I had always possessed that comes with the territory of being a Jehovah's Witness.

After decades of witnessing the "Witnesses," I could now see the truth about "The Truth."

Then, for the first time in my life, I was able to have a fulfilling, loving, and peaceful marriage.

For the first time in my life, I gained friends who loved me back, unconditionally.

For the first time in my life, I was truly happy and not living in daily guilt.

To my delight and amazement, I found that my real journey to God's House was just beginning.

But that's another story.

Brock Talon

☆

Also available from Brock Talon

Escape from Paradise:

Leaving Jehovah's Witnesses and the Watch Tower after thirty-five years of lost dreams

A memoir

An innocent child named Brock Talon longs for the Jehovah's Witness paradise, but in time finds it isn't all it's cracked up to be. With Armageddon ever looming, his life becomes an endless stream of restrictions and mandated works, harsh discipline and conditional relationships.

Join Brock's struggle with apostasy and persecution, sanctioned abuse and God-like elders. Learn with him about his faith's built-in sexual dysfunction and an eerily business-like design, as well as its dubious origin, repeated failed prophecy, fixation on demons, and the curious "anointed ones." Will Brock ignore his eye-opening discoveries, or will he act and lose everything?

This story, both humorous and tragic, is about one man's personal pilgrimage through the dystopian world of the Watch Tower Bible and Tract Society. Along with millions like him, will Brock be able to safely make his escape from paradise?

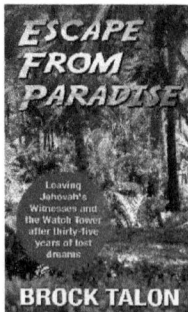

⭐

The Redemption Sect

A novel

Blake Vanguard, ex-Navy SEAL and entrepreneur, is unable to come to terms with the circumstances of his wife's horrific death. Using his military fighting skills, he seeks revenge on the organization he blames for her untimely demise - The Church of Consummate Redemption.

Having lost everything over his obsession, Blake is reduced to mundane private detective work before a beautiful woman with a tragic story hires him. The case he takes on clashes with the local police who are investigating a string of mutilations and gruesome deaths. With the clues piling up, it appears that an apocalyptic religious order may be responsible for these heinous acts.

As the stakes rise with each passing day, the mystery grows to one of international proportions. Will Blake succumb to his inner demon, or can he decipher the true meaning of what he faces before it is too late?

www.ingramcontent.com/pod-product-compliance
Lightning Source LLC
Chambersburg PA
CBHW060236050426
42448CB00009B/1463